Global Business Case Studies

Yasuo Nakatani   Ryan Smithers

JN061743

SEIBIDO

photographs by

Shutterstock

森永製菓㈱

㈱良品計画

花王㈱

本田技研工業㈱

㈱八ちゃん堂

㈱帝国ホテル

㈱田代合金所

ヤマハ発動機㈱

Twitter Japan㈱

アイ・シー・ネット㈱

音声ファイルのダウン / ストリーミング

CD マークがある箇所は、音声を弊社 HP より無料でダウンロード / ストリーミングすることができます。下記 URL の書籍詳細ページに音声ダウンロードアイコンがございますのでそちらから自習用音声としてご活用ください。

https://www.seibido.co.jp/ad664

Global Business Case Studies

はじめに

●興味深いビジネス英語の内容理解をTOEIC形式の問題で楽しく学べる

　TOEICテストで高得点を目指すには、ビジネスの基礎知識も必要となります。本書の問題演習の多くは、TOEICの出題形式に沿って構成されています。グローバルリーダーに関する重要な事象を扱ったケースを通して学んだビジネス英語の成果をTOEIC形式で確認できます。単なる資格試験のための勉強ではなく、本来の重要なビジネス英語の基礎を楽しく学ぶことが可能になります。これらの学習を通してTOEICの成績アップだけでなく、それぞれの企業や業界も学べるので就職活動にも役立つことでしょう。

●臨場感あふれる国際ビジネスのケースでリーダーシップと交渉を学ぶ

　グローバルリーダーになるためには、どのような条件が必要なのでしょうか。本書は日本の代表的な企業などにおける実際の15のビジネスケースを取り扱い、国際社会で活躍を目指す人のロールモデルを示しています。英語学習を通して、リーダーシップとは何か、それをどのように身に付け、いかに発揮すべきかを実例で学んでいきます。

　全ての章の内容は、筆者が直接インタビューを行い作成したケーススタディに基づいています。このため、単なる企業の歴史や概要ではなく、グローバル化が進む中で、実際に起こった困難なミッションに対して、当事者が必死になってリーダーシップを発揮した臨場感あふれる内容となっています。

●もしあなたがリーダーなら、次のようなグローバルな課題をどう解決するか?

　もし、あなたがタイ資生堂の代表となって赴任したら、どのように若者にブランドを浸透させていくでしょうか。米国花王のビオレの販売がうまくいかない状況で、マーケティングリーダー担当となった時、どのように対応すればよいでしょう。東南アジアでサムソンなどの韓国企業にテレビ販売のシェアを奪われてしまったら、どのような起死回生の戦略をうつべきでしょう。アフリカで清潔な水を手に入れられない地域の人々に、どのような支援が可能でしょうか。

　本書では、その他いくつものケースを英語で学び、自分はどのようにリーダーシップを発揮すべきなのか考えていきます。リーダーに必要な決断力や、コミットメントの仕方を疑似体験しながら身に付けることができます。

●ビジネスや経営の基礎知識を英語で楽しく学ぶ

　マーケティングや経営戦略、日本発のラグジュアリービジネス、さらに近年注目の高いSDGs (Sustainable Development Goals)に関する、英語のビジネス語句およびコンセプトを、実際にあった興味深いケースで学ぶことで自然に理解ができるようになります。

本書の効果的な使い方

　このテキストは、これまで明らかになっている有効な学習ストラテジー理論を取り入れています。

▶ Business Issue　ビジネスの課題を把握する

ビジネスケースの背景知識を日本語で理解し、英語学習の準備をします。各リーダーが解決しなければならない問題を日本語で興味深く提示しています。

▶ Warm-up　写真を見て状況を聞き取る問題

談話の理解を高めるためには、事前に画像などで関連する知識（スキーマ）を活性化することが有効とされています。まずケースに関連する写真描写問題や、応答問題を通して学習の準備をしましょう。TOEICのPart1の形式に慣れていきます。

▶ Vocabulary Input　語彙トレーニング

談話理解のための詳細な下方向からの情報のインプットを行います。ケースの理解に必要な重要語句の意味を理解していきます。

▶ Learning Important Expressions for Business Case Studies

ケースの理解に必要な語句や文法知識を身につけるため、TOEIC Part5形式で練習します。

▶ Listening Booster　ビジネスの背景を学ぼう！　聴解トレーニング

A. ケースで取り扱う企業の基本情報に関するビジネス英語の音声に慣れます。
　聴解トレーニングとしてTOEICのPart3、Part4の形式によって内容を聞き取り理解するトレーニングを行います。
B. ディクテーションで重要な語句を聞き取り、英語で企業情報を把握する練習をします。
　Aの復習として音声の英文を確認し内容理解の定着を目指します。

▶ Learning From Authentic Business Examples　読解トレーニング

臨場感あふれる企業ケースの内容を理解します。ケースの前提となる状況を英語で読み解きます。ここは読解のスキミング、スキャニングのトレーニングとして、正誤問題で英文の内容理解を確認します。

Reading Booster　読解力をより高めるトレーニング

いよいよ各リーダーたちが問題解決能力を最大限発揮し、困難に立ち向かいます。皆さんも自分の立場に置き換えて解決方法を考えてください。少し長めの英文で読解のスキャニング、スキミング・トレーニングも行い、TOEIC Part7 の形式で理解を確認します。

Notes
ビジネス知識のあまりない学習者は、事前に語句を日本語で確認しておきましょう。

Tasks for Business Studies

A Business Focus
ケースを理解するのに必要となる、グローバルビジネスで重要なマーケティングや戦略論、交渉術などの基本的な概念を日本語で学びます。企業や業界研究の促進や就職活動にも役立ちます。

B ビジネス英語の理解を深めよう！
Aで学んだマーケティングや戦略論、交渉術などに関して、本文の英文ケースの具体的な事例を通して確認します。空所補充のタスクで内容を再度復習し、次のCのタスクの準備をします。

C Business Discussion
ペアやグループになり英語で話し合い、内容を書いてまとめる練習をします。
英文を書く練習をして、各章で学んだビジネス英語の最後にもう一度定着させます。

Review Unit 1-4
各ユニットのビジネスケースを復習し、TOEIC　Part2，Part6，Part7の形式で理解の定着を行います。

CONTENTS

UNIT
1

Global Marketings

Marketing Mix in Emerging Countries

Shiseido Thailand

Shiseido has established a global megabrand through success in emerging markets.

資生堂は化粧品のグローバル・メガブランドである。今や 120 の国と地域でビジネスを展開している。2020 年に資生堂の年間売上高は約 1.2 兆円になり、そのうち約 60% は海外ビジネスである。しかしながら 1990 年代半ばまでは、海外の売り上げは 10%に満たなかった。急成長には新興国での発展が欠かせなかった。特にグローバル市場で最も成功しているのは中国である。また近年急成長を遂げているのは東南アジアで毎年 8% から 10% も発展している。

Business Issue 新興国市場の戦略モデルの構築

　資生堂タイランドの社長に赴任した山田は、度重なる政情不安や自然災害に遭遇し、困難なビジネス環境を切り抜けていかなければならなかった。さらに、ブランドは高品質としてタイの富裕層には支持されていたが、高価な製品というイメージもあり、若い女性にはそれほど人気がない。数々の問題解決のためには、現地の人々への積極的なコミュニケーション戦略を実施するしかなかった。

Warm-up

写真に関する英文を聞き学習の準備をしましょう。最も適切な選択肢を選びましょう。 1-02

(A)　　(B)　　(C)　　(D)

Vocabulary Input

次の英語に合う日本語を選び記号で答えましょう。 1-03

1. net sales　　　　　　　（　　）
2. incorporate　　　　　　（　　）
3. distribution channels　（　　）
4. corporate culture　　　（　　）
5. management asset　　　（　　）
6. passion for beauty　　　（　　）
7. Japanese hospitality　　（　　）

(A) 企業文化	(B) 経営資源	(C) 美に対する情熱	(D) 売上高
(E) おもてなし	(F) 流通チャネル	(G) 取り込む	

Learning Important Expressions for Business Case Studies

ケースの理解に重要な表現に関連する下記の英文を完成させましょう。

1. The Thai workers were ------- and almost never disagreed with supervisors.

   (A) harmony   (B) obedient   (C) requiring   (D) substitute

2. He operates many large retail businesses such as -------.

   (A) stands   (B) banks   (C) hypermarkets   (D) clinics

3. Because of unexpected delays, delivery will not be possible ------- the end of the month.

   (A) by   (B) over   (C) of   (D) to

Listening Booster

企業情報に関する英文を聞いて背景を理解しましょう。   1-04

A. Listen and choose the best answer to each question.

1. When did Shiseido start its business?

   (A) In 1972   (B) In 1902   (C) In 1872   (D) In 2017

2. How many countries does Shiseido operate its business in?

   (A) 19   (B) 20   (C) 100   (D) 120

3. What percentage of Shiseido's business is operated overseas?

   (A) 10   (B) 16   (C) 60   (D) 90

B. Listening Review

Aの音声をもう一度聞き下の英文の（　　　　）に適切な表現を書き入れましょう。   1-05

Long History in Japanese-style Cosmetic Business

In 1872, Japan's first Western-style pharmacy opened in the Tokyo Ginza [1](   ). The name of that company was Shiseido. However, Shiseido soon changed from a [2](   ) to a cosmetics company. It can be said that Shiseido's success depends on their corporate [3](   ), which has always been about providing high quality services and products to customers. Moreover, their business culture includes the Japanese hospitality concept of *omotenashi*. In fact, Shiseido's corporate culture is a management

⁴(   ) that has allowed the company to expand their business in the world. Now, the company operates in approximately 120 countries and regions around the world, with 60 percent of their total sales coming from foreign markets.

▶ **Learning From Authentic Business Examples**

資生堂のビジネスケースに関する英文レポートを読んで後の問いに答えましょう。　 1-06,07

GLOBAL BUSINESS

Becoming a Global Shiseido

The growth of the southeast Asian market is being influenced by Thailand. The Thais have a strong passion for beauty. Shiseido understood the huge business potential of the Thai market from 1962, the year when the company started selling cosmetics in Thailand.

5　When Masato Yamada was appointed President of Shiseido Thailand, he started organizing about 300 local Thai employees. He needed to incorporate Shiseido's unique Japanese corporate culture into Thai working conditions. For example, because Thai people respect harmony and friendly relationships, the workers were very accommodating. This

10　was sometimes beneficial at offices. However, the Thai workers were often too obedient and almost never disagreed with their supervisors. Consequently, they were afraid to report bad news or problems, which made it difficult for Yamada to know the truth about some of the frequent political problems that occurred in Thailand.

Notes

・**accommodating** やさしい　・**obedient** 従順な　・**supervisors** 上司や管理者

本文の内容として正しい場合は T を、正しくない場合は F を（　）に書きましょう。

1. Mr. Yamada needed to incorporate unique aspects of Thai culture into Shiseido's corporate culture. （　　）

2. Thai employees rarely disagree with their boss. （　　）

3. Mr. Yamada was unable to know the truth about some political problems in Thailand. （　　）

次の Shiseido のビジネスケースを読んで質問に答えましょう。　1-08〜11

Enhancing Masstige Marketing in Thailand

　　Due to the political problems and natural disasters that often occurred in Thailand, Yamada had a tough time predicting sales figures and managing Shiseido's inventory. He had to communicate with his Thai staff and local stakeholders to get honest news about the mood of the Thai people. At first, this was difficult, but eventually, Yamada was able to develop many friendships. This enabled him to have the valuable 5 support he needed for Shiseido to survive in Thailand.

　　To expand the business, Shiseido could not rely on only the rich for sales. Yamada needed to make Shiseido popular with younger people, and people who had low or middle incomes. To achieve this goal, Yamada canceled the contract with local agents and controlled the company's promotion directly. He believed that if Shiseido 10 promoted a product line called Za by a marketing mix strategy, he could gain a greater market share in Thailand.

　　The first step that Yamada took was to ask the Shiseido research center to develop a new Za skincare product for the Thai women. His next step was to arrange for a line of Za products to be priced cheaply for younger people. Unfortunately, masstige 15 marketing did not go well for Shiseido because it did not have relevant relationships with hypermarkets. Yamada needed to find new distribution channels, and he managed to do so. His successful negotiations at the head offices of mega-hypermarket stores such as Tesco Lotus and Big C Supermarket gave consumers easier access to Za products. Lastly, Yamada hired a young Thai superstar to be the brand ambassador, which created 20 familiarity between Thai people and Za products.

　　Consequently, Yamada was able to achieve success because of effective communication strategies that respected the local culture and customers. Shiseido's net sales doubled, and its local staff grew from 300 to 700. Furthermore, by 2016, Shiseido had attracted more younger customers, with 40 percent of its total portfolio coming 25 from Thai customers under the age of 30.

Notes

・ **masstige** 大衆向けよりは高級感があるがプレミアムより値ごろ感がある製品
・ **Za** 資生堂が中国やアジア・オセアニアで展開していた中低価格帯の化粧品ブランド
・ **brand ambassador** ブランドを代表する有名人　・ **portfolio** 売上構成

1. Why did Yamada need to spend a lot of time and effort to talk with his Thai staff?

    (A) Because they were politicians.

    (B) Because they had knowledge of the weather.

    (C) Because they delivered the local newspapers.

    (D) Because they knew how Thais felt about things.

2. Who helped Shiseido to make Za products popular with Thai people?

    (A) a superstar

    (B) a customer

    (C) Yamada's competitor

    (D) Yamada's friend

3. How did Shiseido improve its business by 2016?

    (A) The number of employees doubled since its products launched.

    (B) Its net sales increased 300 percent from the previous year.

    (C) Younger people under the age of 30 became its main customers.

    (D) A Thai politician agreed to become the brand ambassador of Shiseido.

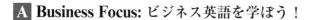
A Business Focus: ビジネス英語を学ぼう！

Marketing Mix : マーケティングで重要な要素である以下の４Ｐの要素を状況に応じて最適化して成功を目指す戦略

Product : 市場に最も合った製品を開発する

Price : 顧客に最適な価格を設定する

Place : 顧客にとって最も商品を入手しやすい方法で販売する

Promotion : 顧客に最も効果的な宣伝や PR を行う

B ビジネス英語の理解を深めよう！

Marketing Mixに関する以下の例文を与えられた文字に続くように空所をうめて完成させましょう。この際、本文を再度確認し、関連する他の事象にも下線を引き **C** のタスクにも活用できるようにしましょう。

1. For the (*p*　　　　　) strategy, the manger asked the research center to (*d*　　　　)
   a new product line for (*l*　　　　) customers.

2. For the (*p*　　　　　) strategy, the manager (*a*　　　　) for new products to be
   priced (*c*　　　　) for younger people.

3. For the (*p*　　　　　) strategy, the manager needed to (*f*　　　　) new distribution
   (*c*　　　　).

4. For the (*p*　　　　　) strategy, the manger used a young Thai (*s*　　　　) to create
   (*f*　　　　) with local consumers.

C Business Discussion

Bの表現を参考にして、次のテーマについてクラスメートと話し合いましょう。

How did Shiseido Thailand implement its marketing mix strategies?

1. Product

_____

_____

2. Price

_____

_____

3. Place

_____

_____

4. Promotion

_____

_____

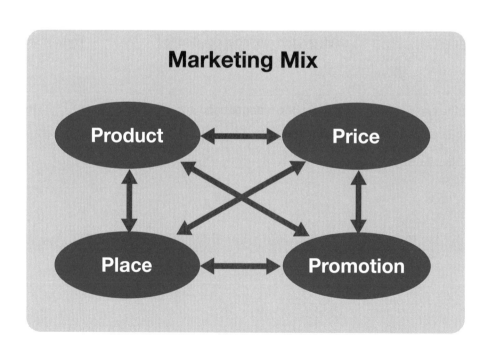

Confectionery Marketing in Overseas Business

Morinaga America, Inc.

Recently, Morinaga has raised the brand recognition by using sports marketing strategies.

　森永製菓は 1889 年に創業された製菓企業である。1914 年には森永ミルクキャラメルを発売し大成功を収めた。さらに消費者に寄り添う形で 1936 年に母の日のキャンペーンを始めた。また、1960 年にはバレンタインデーにチョコレートを贈るというプロモーション活動を始めた。1975 年には最初のハイチュウを発売している。このように日本では有数の企業として発展したが海外進出は遅れており、いかにグローバルな展開をしていくのかが課題であった。

Business Issue　米国人に日本のお菓子を広める

　森永製菓は日本を代表するお菓子メーカーである。だが海外では文化や味の好みなどが異なるためグローバル化は進んでいなかった。2000 年からハワイでハイチュウが売れ始めたのを機に、米国本土でも本格的な販売を目指した。2008 年に米国森永製菓（株）を設立し、カリフォルニア州の市場から開拓することを目指した。だが森永の認知度は低く、アジア食品を取り扱うスーパーの一部で販売されているだけであった。2013 年に米国森永の CEO に赴任した星野はハイチュウを全米に拡げるために新たなマーケティング戦略を試みた。

Warm-up

写真に関する英文を聞き学習の準備をしましょう。最も適切な選択肢を選びましょう。　🎧 1-12

　　　　　　　　　　　　　　　　　　　(A)　　(B)　　(C)　　(D)

Vocabulary Input

次の英語に合う日本語を選び記号で答えましょう。　🎧 1-13

1. nutritious　　　　　　　　(　　　)
2. confectionery　　　　　　(　　　)
3. texture　　　　　　　　　(　　　)
4. brand recognition　　　　(　　　)
5. overseas subsidiaries　　(　　　)
6. the total sales　　　　　(　　　)
7. retail and wholesale　　(　　　)

> (A) 触感　　　　(B) 総売り上げ　　(C) ブランドの認知　　(D) お菓子
> (E) 栄養のある　(F) 小売と卸売　　(G) 海外子会社

Learning Important Expressions for Business Case Studies

ビジネスケースの理解に重要な表現に関連する下記の英文を完成させましょう。

1. Milk Caramel became an enormous hit ------- its excellent taste.

   (A) because   (B) as   (C) since   (D) because of

2. HI-CHEW's texture and fruit flavors were well ------- by Americans.

   (A) distinguished   (B) received   (C) organized   (D) introduced

3. Only a few retailers considered ------- their products.

   (A) having stocked   (B) to stock   (C) stocking   (D) would stock

Listening Booster

森永に関するチャットを聞いて質問に答えましょう。   CD 1-14

A. Listen and choose the best answer to each question.

1. When was Morinaga founded?

   (A) 1889   (B) 1914   (C) 1975   (D) 2020

2. Approximately, how many fruit-flavored products has Morinaga developed until now?

   (A) 14   (B) 165   (C) 2,711   (D) 2 billion

B. Listening Review

Aの音声をもう一度聞き下の英文の（   ）に適切な表現を書き入れましょう。   CD 1-15

Jane Brown (11: 00 AM)

Let's discuss the secret of Morinaga's success.

Dick Johnson (11: 02 AM)

I found that since the company's founding in 1889, Morinaga & Co. has worked to create a positive company culture.

Jane Brown (11: 07 AM)

I know that they provide delicious and highly nutritious Western [1](   ) to Japanese consumers.

Dick Johnson (11: 10 AM)

That is true. For example, in 1914, they launched the pocket-sized Milk Caramel, which became an enormous hit because of its excellent taste and [2](   ).

Jane Brown (11: 16 AM)

Another good example is a chewy candy called HI-CHEW, isn't it? The company ³(   ) a strawberry-flavored HI-CHEW in 1975. Since then, they have developed more than 165 different fruit-flavored products.

Dick Johnson (11: 20 AM)

No wonder they experienced huge success. Their net sales ⁴(   ) more than 2 billion yen in 2020, and they had more than 2,711 employees and overseas subsidiaries in five countries.

Learning From Authentic Business Examples

森永のビジネスケースに関する英文を読んで後の問いに答えましょう。   1-16,17

Enhancing Overseas Business

     Morinaga & Co.'s overseas sales were only a small percentage of the company's total sales. Expansion to America for Morinaga & Co. seemed to have great potential because of a survey that showed how much Americans love candy. In fact, Americans eat an average of 40 kilograms of candy a year. Some Japanese
5 trading companies exported HI-CHEW to the U.S. HI-CHEW was becoming popular in Hawaii by 2000. Noticing the potential for sales in America, Morinaga & Co. sampled this market and learned that HI-CHEW's texture and fruit flavors were unique and well received by Americans. This led to the beginning of operations in California and the establishment of Morinaga America, Inc. in August 2008.
10   Morinaga America initially tried to expand from Asian retail channels such as Japanese and Korean supermarkets who had been importing product from Japan. As these shops had already sold HI-CHEW, their consumers could accept the product easily. Following this, the company attempted to penetrate the main retail channels in the U.S., such as large supermarket chains, convenience stores, and
15 other major food stores. However, as there was low brand recognition, few retailers considered stocking HI-CHEW. In fact, it was very difficult for Morinaga America representatives to make appointments with these stores. Eventually though, Costco agreed to deal with Morinaga and sell HI-CHEW at some of their stores in California.

Notes

· **Costco** 大型会員制ディスカウントチェーン

本文の内容として正しい場合は T を、正しくない場合は F を（　）に書きましょう。

1. Initially, some Japanese trading companies exported HI-CHEW to America.　（　　）

2. Considering the results of the sample survey, Morinaga America, Inc. was established in August 2008.　（　　）

3. Quite a few retailers considered stocking HI-CHEW.　（　　）

> **Reading Booster**

次の Morinaga のビジネスケースを読んで質問に答えましょう。　 1-18～20

Successful Consumer Marketing in the U.S.

　　　　Mr. Masao Hoshino was appointed CEO of Morinaga America in 2013 to establish HI-CHEW as a strong confectionery brand there. He found it was necessary to use leading confectionery brokers who have special connections for selling manufacturers' products to the retail and wholesale trade. Hoshino visited several companies and exhibited at confectionery exhibitions to find regional brokers who 5 could effectively introduce new products to the markets and optimize promotional activities such as securing strategic shelf space. However, when the brokers did not perform as expected, Morinaga canceled the contract and appointed another broker to maintain the most effective sales channel to retailers.

　　　　In 2012, Mr. Junichi Tazawa, who played Major League Baseball for the Boston 10 Red Sox, asked Morinaga to send him HI-CHEW. Whenever he brought HI-CHEW to the bullpen, he shared it with his teammates. As Morinaga sent Tazawa HI-CHEW on a regular basis, he promoted the product to his teammates to show Morinaga his appreciation. Since then, Morinaga became an official sponsor of other Major League teams such as the Chicago Cubs and Minnesota Twins. Morinaga also signed sponsorship 15 agreements with the New York Knicks of the National Basketball Association. As a result of these sports marketing strategies, which are very effective in America, Morinaga raised the brand recognition for HI-CHEW.

20 Morinaga realized that marketing campaigns that offered free samples of HI-CHEW worked with younger people. As a result, Morinaga now supports athletic programs for young people. For example, it provided more than 7,000 HI-CHEW candies to football programs at schools in northern Utah and Los Angeles. These localization marketing strategies succeeded, and the sales of HI-CHEW increased from 400 million yen in 2011 to 6.4 billion yen in 2020. Now in the U.S., 1.98 million pieces 25 of HI-CHEW are being eaten every day and almost 700 million pieces per year.

Notes

· **confectionery brokers** 菓子類を専門に扱うブローカー　·**strategic shelf space** 売れる商品を陳列する棚
· **Junichi Tazawa** 田澤純一：ボストン・レッドソックスで活躍した投手
· **Major League Baseball** 米国大リーグ　·**bullpen** 投手が集まる登板前の投球練習場
· **Chicago Cubs and Minnesota Twins** 米国大リーグのシカゴ・カブス、ミネソタ・ツインズ
· **New York Knicks of the National Basketball Association** 米国プロバスケットボールのニューヨーク・ニックス　·**Utah** ユタ州　·**Los Angeles** カリフォルニア州のロス・アンゼルス

1. Why was Mr. Hoshino appointed as the CEO of Morinaga America?

   (A) because he liked eating HI-CHEW

   (B) because he was a team player

   (C) because he was asked to make HI-CHEW popular in the U.S.

   (D) because he was good at sports

2. Why did Morinaga cancel contracts with regional brokers?

   (A) because they ate up the profits

   (B) because they did a poor job

   (C) because they optimized promotional activities

   (D) because they targeted younger people

3. Which sports marketing strategy did Morinaga NOT try?

   (A) a sponsorship agreement with the Knicks

   (B) giving away free candy to young athletes

   (C) providing HI-CHEW to Tazawa

   (D) giving free samples to school baseball teams in Utah

A **Business Focus:** ビジネス英語を学ぼう！

A. Business Focus: ビジネス英語を学ぼう！

- Using Confectionery Brokers for Developing Retail Channels

  米国では、主要な流通チャネルで商品を取り扱ってもらうには実力のあるブローカーと契約する必要がある。彼らは販売促進や有利な売り場の獲得のコンサルティングも行う。

- Marketing Through Sports in the U.S.

  米国はスポーツがとても盛んであり、特に３大スポーツと呼ばれるアメリカン・フットボール、ベースボール、バスケットボールは人気がある。これらのイベントに関連したマーケティング活動はとても効果がある。

B ビジネス英語の理解を深めよう！

Marketing Strategy に関する以下の例文を与えられた文字に続くように空所をうめて完成させましょう。この際、本文を再度確認し、関連する他の事象にも下線を引き **C** のタスクにも活用できるようにしましょう。

1. In the U.S., it is essential to select relevant (b   ) who have special (c   ) for selling manufacturers' products to the major retail and (w   ) trade.

2. Because sports are an important part of American (c   ), sporting events and sports (t   ) can be an excellent marketing opportunity to (p   ) products in the U.S.

3. The company supports (a   ) programs for young people and offers free (s   ) of HI-CHEW.

C Business Discussion

B の表現を参考にして以下の質問をクラスメートと話し合いましょう。

Why was Morinaga successful at promoting HI-CHEW?

1. Developing distribution channels

_____

_____

2. Marketing through major league sports

_____

_____

3. Marketing for young people

_____

_____

Three Major Sports

Exploring Global Business and Enhancing People's Sustainable Value

Chapter 3

MUJI : Ryohin Keikaku

MUJI
無印良品

MUJI has established strong and consistent global strategies.

　無印良品は 1980 年にスーパーマーケットチェーンの西友のプライベートブランドとして登場した。「わけあって、安い」というコンセプトを打ち出し、バブル経済に酔い贅沢品を浪費する消費者に素材の本質の価値を再認識させた。1989 年に西友から良品計画として独立して以降、デザインや商品の価値が認められビジネスは急激な成長を見せた。順調な同社の発展も 2001 年に滞り状況が悪化したため、斬新な改善策を導入するしかなかった。また同様に、海外店舗展開戦略の大幅な見直しをした。これらの努力が功を奏し、2021 年良品計画のグローバルの店舗数は 1,002 店舗に拡大し、合計 4,536 億円の営業収益を上げている。

Business Issue 中国・アジア市場の開拓

　良品計画は香港やシンガポールにも早い時期から進出していたが、様々な困難に直面し1998年にアジアから撤退した。また、中国においても登録商標の問題などで、十分な展開ができなかった。西友のアジア事業部長を務めていた松﨑は、製品のグローバルな価値を認識しており、2001年に西友のテナントとして香港に再出店を依頼した。また2003年にはシンガポールでも同様に再出店を支援した。良品計画は、2002年に西友がウォルマート傘下に入り、将来ウォルマートの子会社になることを受けて、2004年に西友が保有する香港の株式を買い取り完全に独立した。松﨑も西友の海外事業の整理に目処がついたため、良品計画に移籍し、グローバル化を推し進める。大きな成長が望める中国市場でのビジネス拡大を計画したが、複雑な商習慣や契約制度など様々な困難を乗り越えなければならなかった。

Warm-up

写真に関する英文を聞き学習の準備をしましょう。最も適切な選択肢を選びましょう。 1-21

(A)　　(B)　　(C)　　(D)

Vocabulary Input

次の英語に合う日本語を選び記号で答えましょう。 1-22

1. currency crisis 　　（　　）
2. prioritize 　　（　　）
3. close business 　　（　　）
4. rental contracts 　　（　　）
5. consistent strategies 　　（　　）
6. turnover rent 　　（　　）
7. liquidation 　　（　　）
8. age and isolate 　　（　　）

(A) 商売をやめる	(B) 一貫した戦略	(C) 売上歩合制の賃料	(D) 通貨危機
(E) 清算	(F) 賃貸契約	(G) 高齢になる過疎になる	(H) 優先する

ビジネスケースの理解に重要な表現に関連する下記の英文を完成させなさい。

1. Partners have recognized MUJI's high brand power ------- to the company's great success in China.

(A) directly   (B) payable   (C) up   (D) due

2. He was ------- of the need to build strong global consistent strategies.

(A) in charge   (B) convinced   (C) trying   (D) in front

3. The company believes in being ------- to the lives of ordinary people.

(A) closer   (B) finished   (C) remote   (D) middle

▶ Listening Booster ▮▮

企業情報に関する英文を聞いて背景を理解しましょう。 1-23

A. Listen and choose the best answer to each question.

1. When did MUJI withdraw from Asian countries?

(A) In 1988

(B) In 1989

(C) In 1998

(D) In 2002

2. Who was Mr. Matsuzaki?

(A) The marketing manager of MUJI

(B) The top manager of a joint venture in China

(C) The top executive of MUJI Hong Kong

(D) The general manager of Seiyu's overseas business

3. What was mentioned about Walmart?

(A) It was taken over by MUJI.

(B) Mr. Matsuzaki was put in charge of it.

(C) It had to leave the Asian market.

(D) It caused problems with the Seiyu and MUJI joint venture.

B. Listening Review

Ａの音声をもう一度聞き下の英文の（　　　　）に適切な表現を書き入れましょう。　 CD 1-24

A: I found that MUJI had withdrawn from Asian countries in 1998.

B: Really? I thought it was a strong brand there.

A: That was true, but because of the Asian currency crisis and the company's inadequate joint ¹(　　　　　) the company had to leave the Asian market.

B: How did they ²(　　　　　) the market?

A: Mr. Satoru Matsuzaki, who was the general manager of Seiyu's overseas business division, asked for a MUJI store to be opened in Hong Kong. In fact, he was in charge of ³(　　　　　) the Seiyu Department Store there.

B: I see. So, he wanted to use MUJI to promote Seiyu Department Store, which gave him the idea to set up a joint venture between Ryohin Keikaku and Seiyu.

A: Yes. However, things got very complicated when Seiyu got controlled by the multinational retail chain, Walmart, in 2002.

B: Wow! That would have been a difficult situation to deal with. Especially because Walmart is the world's ⁴(　　　　　) supermarket chain.

> ## Learning From Authentic Business Examples ▮▮▮

良品計画のビジネス記事に関する英文を読んで後の問いに答えましょう。　 CD 1-25〜28

BUSINESS ISSUES　**ECONOMY**

Learning from Walmart

In 2002, Matsuzaki had to make a presentation on future plans for retail business companies in Asia. His presentation was to some representatives from Walmart, the company who controlled Seiyu. The presentation was limited to only one hour. Seiyu's overseas
5 business in Asia has been undergoing structural reforms and liquidation of unprofitable businesses since the late 1990s. And department stores in Hong Kong and Singapore have returned to profitability and are expected to remain profitable. In consideration of this, Mr. Matsuzaki proposed that its overseas business continue in
10 the same way.

Unfortunately, Mr. Matsuzaki's proposal was not accepted at the meeting. At that time, Matsuzaki learned that a global company like Walmart must prioritize its own management strategy and business form in doing business worldwide and increasing business profits.
15 After this meeting, Mr. Matsuzaki was busy working to dissolve Seiyu's joint ventures and close the Asian businesses one after

another. It was very difficult to withdraw from the businesses because Seiyu had just signed long-term joint ventures or rental contracts with local companies. For example, when closing the business in Thailand, he had to rent an apartment for a year and a half in order 20 to handle the process. Mr. Matsuzaki tried to deal with the closures in good faith so that he could reduce the damage to the other parties as much as possible. Moreover, he wanted Seiyu's partners to be successful after Seiyu left. In July 2005, since almost all the business liquidation processes were coming to an end, Matsuzaki was 25 transferred to Ryohin Keikaku.

Seiyu's closures caused a lot of trouble with stakeholders and sadness for Mr. Matsuzaki. He promised never to fail in any overseas business in the future. He knew Ryohin Keikaku would need to have strong global strategies, like Walmart's, so that the company could 30 compete globally.

Notes

· **Walmart** 世界最大のスーパーマーケットで Everyday Low Price を方針にしている
· **in good faith** 誠意を持って
· **trouble with stakeholders** 合弁事業の解消やテナント契約の解約による不利益

本文の内容として正しい場合は T を、正しくない場合は F を（　）に書きましょう。

1. Seiyu successfully ran its business in the form of a department store in Asia.　（　　）

2. Walmart accepted the proposal for Seiyu's overseas business to continue in the same way.　（　　）

3. Mr. Matsuzaki terminated the overseas business with Walmart in 2005.　（　　）

Reading Booster

次の Ryohin Keikaku のビジネスケースを読んで質問に答えましょう。 CD 1-29〜33

From Global to Local

In 2005, Mr. Matsuzaki became the General Manager of Asia Operations and he was appointed as General Manager of China Business in 2008. In China, growth can be expected, but business practices are complex and tenant rents are soaring. With this understanding of the Chinese market, Mr. Matsuzaki developed a consistent strategy for negotiations with Chinese developers and landlords. He made contracts on the basis 5 of a turnover rent. That is, Ryohin Keikaku would pay only a percentage rent based on gross sales. If these conditions could not be agreed to after two rounds of negotiations, Mr. Matsuzaki would end negotiations and look for another place to rent. Fortunately, many Chinese business partners knew of MUJI's high brand power due to the company's success in Shanghai and Beijing. This made it easier to negotiate these strict rent conditions. Mr. Matsuzaki and his subordinate implemented this consistent strategy and opened 200 stores. Surprisingly, they did this work by themselves to reduce management costs. In 2021, there were 299 stores in Mainland China, which accounted for more than half of MUJI's 546 overseas stores.

Between 2000 and 2015, it was only in 2013 that the number of customers exceeded its counterpart in the previous year in Japan. Thus, when Mr. Matsuzaki became CEO of Ryohin Keikaku in 2015, he redefined the company's values. That is, he aimed to have the company's activities be closer to the lives of customers. As a result, the company reduced the prices of items so that more people could buy MUJI products that are useful in daily life. The first step was to lower the price of its popular socks in 2016.

This strategy worked effectively and expanded MUJI's customer traffic. From fiscal 2016, the number of customers has remained a positive increase year on year. In fiscal 2019, Ryohin Keikaku recorded a double digit increase in customer traffic, and this also contributed to the increase in revenue.

In line with MUJI's aim, the company started supporting people living in many rural areas in Japan. Because some towns have an aging population and are isolated, Ryohin Keikaku opened shops in cooperation with local companies. Also, they started the MUJI to Go mobile sales by bus service to sell daily necessities to people living in remote areas.

One cutting-edge example of Ryohin Keikaku's efforts to be closer to customers is MUJI Naoetsu in Niigata. There, the people were greatly inconvenienced when a major supermarket closed its big shopping center. Ryohin Keikaku saw this as an opportunity and after discussions with the local stakeholders, they opened one of the world's biggest MUJI stores in 2020.

Notes

· **tenant rents are soaring** 上昇するテナント賃料
· **MUJI to Go** ミニバスで過疎地に訪問販売するサービス
· **MUJI Naoetsu** 新潟県直江津にある５千平方メートルの巨大ショッピングセンター。大手スーパーが撤退した後に良品計画が出店

1. When the rent conditions were not met, what did Mr. Matsuzaki do?

   (A) He proposed that the parties develop a future relationship.

   (B) He continued negotiations because of his desire to open a new store.

   (C) He followed his consistent strategy and ended negotiations.

   (D) He demonstrated the value of MUJI's high brand power.

2. How many stores in China was Mr. Matsuzaki directly involved in opening?

   (A) 200   (B) 299   (C) 546   (D) More than half

3. Why did Ryohin Keikaku launch a business in Naoetsu?

   (A) They were looking for business opportunities at one of the world's biggest malls.

   (B) Many people living in remote areas wanted a new MUJI shop nearby.

   (C) They predicted that a price reduction strategy could help local people.

   (D) They followed their aim to support the lives of people who lived in rural areas.

Tasks for Business Studies

A Business Focus: ビジネス英語を学ぼう！

Establishing strong and consistent global strategies for global business
グローバルな競争に勝つには強力な世界共通の戦略を確立する必要がある。

Being closer to the lives of ordinary people
良品計画の企業理念の一つは人々の暮らしに寄り添う製品サービスの提供である。

MUJI to Go mobile sales by bus service
過疎地に住む高齢者などの生活必需品を買えない地域の人のためにミニバスで定期的に訪問販売をしている。

B ビジネス英語の理解を深めよう！

良品計画に関する以下の例文を与えられた文字に続くように空所をうめて完成させましょう。この際、本文を再度確認し、関連する他の事象にも下線を引き C のタスクにも活用できるようにしましょう。

1. Mr. Matsuzaki (r   ) the need to have Ryohin Keikaku (c   ) globally with strong global (s   ), like Walmart's.

2. Mr. Matsuzaki treated business (*t*   ) in good faith to reduce the (*d*   ) to other parties as much as (*p*   ).

3. Ryohin Keikaku supports people who are (*a*   ) and isolated in many (*r*   ) areas in Japan.

4. Thanks to MUJI, the local (*c*   ) of Naoetsu can enjoy a (*s*   ) lifestyle.

C Business Discussion

B の表現を参考にして、次のテーマについてクラスメートと話し合いましょう。

1. What did the leader of Ryohin Keikaku learn from Walmart?

_____

_____

_____

_____

2. When closing a joint venture, what should be done?

_____

_____

_____

_____

3. Why did Ryohin Keikaku start the MUJI to Go mobile business?

_____

_____

_____

_____

4. Explain the effect of MUJI's business venture in Naoetsu.

_____

_____

_____

_____

Globalization or Localization

Chapter 4

Kao USA Inc.

Kao

Kao is very good at Management of Technology (MOT).

　花王の創業者の長瀬富郎は日本において衛生的な暮らしを広めるため、1890年に石鹸の販売を開始した。以来、花王は革新的な技術開発に基づき世界の人々の豊かな生活文化の実現を目指して成長してきた。例えば石鹸で何度も顔を洗うと潤い成分が失われる。この問題を解決するために7年の研究の後、1980年にペースト状洗顔料ビオレを開発した。このように花王はMOTという科学技術を応用した製品開発に重きを置く経営手法で成功している。

　今や世界72か国でビジネスを行っている。様々な努力の結果、2020年度の売上高は13,820億円で、営業利益は1,756億円を記録している。

花王ビオレは 1997 年、米国での発売開始の際に、既存の洗顔製品との差別化のため、毛穴まできれいにする技術を訴求した。毛穴パックの商品を導入し、洗浄効果の高いブランドとして一定の顧客を獲得してきた。花王は 2012 年に SPT という高度な肌洗浄化技術を開発し、本社はこれを活用した世界共通戦略の導入を決めた。その際、米国の製品も日本と同様のデザインに変更された。だが、この変更は米国ではうまくいかず、売上も停滞した。米国にマーケティング担当者として赴任した畑瀬は、この状況を何とか打開しなければならなかった。

Warm-up

写真に関する英文を聞き学習の準備をしましょう。最も適切な選択肢を選びましょう。 1-34

(A)　　(B)　　(C)　　(D)

Vocabulary Input

次の英語に合う日本語を選び記号で答えましょう。 1-35

1. customer base （　　）
2. sanitary market （　　）
3. affiliates （　　）
4. charcoal （　　）
5. paste-type （　　）
6. liquid-type （　　）
7. moisture （　　）
8. innovative products （　　）

(A) 顧客基盤 　　(B) 練り物状の 　　(C) 液状の 　　(D) 水分 　　(E) 系列会社

(F) 革新的な製品 　　(G) 炭（すみ） 　　(H) 整髪、洗顔や衛生用品市場

ケースの理解に重要な表現に関連する下記の英文を完成させましょう。

1. Kao provided its original soap at an ------- price.

   (A) avoidable   (B) aggressive   (C) affordable   (D) appointed

2. Bioré has been the ------- product for face washes in Japan.

   (A) problem-solving   (B) top-selling   (C) learner-centered   (D) nature-given

3. Kao headquarters decided to ------- the prestigious local skincare brand, Andrew Jergen.

   (A) face   (B) invent   (C) fight   (D) acquire

Listening Booster

企業情報に関する英文を聞いて背景を理解しましょう。 1-36

A. Listen and choose the best answer to each question.

1. What does Kao want to do for ordinary people?

   (A) share quality trade secrets

   (B) share their top knowledge

   (C) provide innovative sanitary services

   (D) provide reasonable and high-quality facial soap

2. What is the size of Kao's overseas operations?

   (A) It has 87 companies.

   (B) It works in over 70 countries.

   (C) It operates in 17 countries.

   (D) It has expanded to 18 markets.

B. Listening Review

Aの音声をもう一度聞き下の英文の（　　　）に適切な表現を書き入れましょう。 1-37

Improving Consumers' Lives with New Technologies

A: I heard Kao was [1](   ) in 1887 to provide high-quality facial soap for ordinary people at affordable prices.

B: Yes. From the beginning, Kao has been focusing on scientific [2](   ) and [3](   ) for new products.

A: That is why they have achieved the top ⁴(   ) in the Japanese sanitary market.

B: In addition, by producing many ⁵(   ) products, such as Bioré for face washes, Kao has successfully expanded their business.

A: I also use that product. Is Kao famous overseas?

B: Yes, the company has ⁶(   ) in 32 countries and operates business in more than 70 countries.

Learning From Authentic Business Examples

花王のビジネスケースに関する英文を読んで後の問いに答えましょう。 1-38～40

Developing Innovative Skincare and Cleanliness Products With Scientific Approaches

Bioré has become one of the biggest brands for consumers who like to use paste-type cleansers. Another innovative product that Kao created to improve consumers' daily lives was Bioré U body wash. Bioré U body wash is a liquid-type cleanser that changed people's bathing habits.

5   With regard to their overseas business, Kao first launched their products in Asian countries. Kao set up Taiwan–Kao as their first overseas company in 1964, which successfully expanded their customer base in that region. In North America, Kao started their business in 1989. They acquired the local prestigious skincare brand, Andrew Jergen. However, they could not introduce their own products

10   because their brand name was still unfamiliar in American markets. In 1996, Kao developed a new skin care technology which removes the sebum plugs from skin pores like tweezers pulling out a small hair. This product was successful in many countries, so Kao decided to introduce this skin care technology to North America. In 1997, they launched Bioré Pore Strips for nose pore cleansing. It became the top-

15   selling skin care product in the U.S.A.

   As a result, their brand recognition for providing effective skin care increased among American consumers, and Kao USA successfully expanded their business.

Notes

· **sebum plugs** 毛穴に詰まった角栓   · **skin pores** 毛穴   · **tweezers** ピンセット   · **pore strips** 毛穴パック

本文の内容として正しい場合は T を、正しくない場合は F を（　　）に書きましょう。

1. Bioré U body wash is a paste-type cleanser that changed people's bathing habits.

（　　）

2. Kao has operated their business in North America since 1989. （　　）

3. Due to the success of Bioré Pore Strips for nose pore cleansing, Kao was able to develop brand recognition for providing effective skin care products. （　　）

花王 USA のビジネスケースを読んで内容を理解しましょう。　　🔴CD 1-41〜45

Enhancing Glocalization Business Operations

  Strong cleansing products damage the skin by reducing skin moisture. However, in 2012, Kao developed Skin Purifying Technology (SPT). SPT can cleanse the skin thoroughly without damaging it. It is a weak acid that protects the natural pH balance of the skin.

  As SPT technology is so innovative, Kao headquarters decided to launch the 5 Bioré brand globally with a common design, logo, and white and light-blue coloring. The new brand of Bioré using SPT has the same value appeal all over the world. Accordingly, Kao America changed its marketing style and adopted the global communication strategies requested by the headquarters. Unfortunately, the new strategy did not appeal to Americans. As a result, Bioré's total market share in America 10 went down to 3.9 percent.

  In 2013, Takatoshi Hatase became the vice president of Global Marketing in the U.S. He joined the marketing team to improve the Bioré brand. Hatase and his team

reexamined their marketing mix and found several problems. One was that American
15 consumers had already gotten used to using Bioré as an effective pore cleansing product.
It was found that the global format, with its white and light-blue packaging designs, did
not appeal to their American customers.

After struggling to develop new marketing strategies, in 2014, Kao introduced
charcoal-based cleansers with bold white and dark-blue packaging to the U.S. Even
20 though black cleansing products and bold packaging were unfamiliar to U.S. consumers,
Kao created some powerful advertising images to attract consumers and promote this
new product line. In fact, their ads contained women holding heavy-duty machines that
looked like vacuums to show how their product was extra powerful at removing dirt
from women's skin.

25 Such communication strategies to promote the black cleansing product were
different from the global format that used white and light-blue packaging. However, this
strategy greatly appealed to American consumers. In addition, instead of using TV
commercials for advertising, Kao used social media and online platforms to enhance
consumer engagement rates. Such localized communication strategies achieved great
30 success. Their total market share in America increased to 10.4 percent in 2017.

Notes

· **Skin Purifying Technology (SPT)** 花王が開発した肌を傷つけずにきれいにする技術
· **weak acid** 弱酸性　· **natural pH balance** pH（水素イオン濃度指数）が自然な状態
· **heavy-duty machine** 重作業機　· **engagement rate** ユーザーが積極的な反応を示した割合

1. What is unique about the STP cleansing product?

(A) It vacuums the skin.

(B) It protects the pH balance of the skin.

(C) It is made in America.

(D) It contains an acid that can harm the skin.

2. Why didn't the common global strategy appeal to Americans?

(A) It was too expensive.

(B) It didn't work on American skin.

(C) Its design was unappealing to Americans.

(D) The pore cleansing products were too localized.

3. What advertising helped increase Kao's market share in America?

(A) Women with vacuum-like machines

(B) Women with dirty skin

(C) The platform share strategy

(D) The marketing mix campaign

A **Business Focus:** ビジネス英語を学ぼう！

Globalization and Localization
グローバライゼーションは、多国籍企業などが製品やサービスを標準化して、規模の経済などを求めて世界規模で経営の効率化を求める。一方、ローカライゼーションは、各国独自の顧客の消費行動や商習慣に合わせて現地適合化を目指す。

Management of Technology
科学技術を応用して開発した製品やサービスの積極的な活用を経営方針の中心に置き、研究開発に重きを置くことで他社との差別化を行う経営。

B ビジネス英語の理解を深めよう！

花王の戦略に関する以下の例文を、与えられた文字に続くように空所をうめて完成させましょう。この際、本文を再度確認し、関連する他の事象にも下線を引き **C** のタスクにも活用できるようにしましょう。

1. Kao focuses on (*m*　　　　) of (*t*　　　　)(MOT) and has always looked at consumers' daily lives to determine what kinds of (*i*　　　　) products are needed.

2. It (*l*　　　　) Bioré Pore Strips for nose pore cleansing based on MOT in the U.S. (*m*　　　　) in 1997.

3. Kao USA reviewed the (*g*　　　　) strategies requested by the (*h*　　　　) due to a decrease in sales.

4. Then it changed and created powerful (*a*　　　　) images to appeal to American consumers as a (*l*　　　　) strategy in 2014.

C Business Discussion

Bの表現を参考にして、次のテーマについてクラスメートと話し合いましょう。

What kind of marketing strategies has Kao introduced in the North American market?

1. In 1989, _____

   _____

   _____

   _____

2. In 1997, _____

   _____

   _____

   _____

3. In 2012, _____

   _____

   _____

   _____

4. In 2014, _____

   _____

   _____

   _____

Review Unit 1

Chapter1－4 の復習をしましょう

1 最も適切な応答の選択肢を選びましょう。 1-46～49

Listen to the question or statement and three responses. Then choose the best answer.

   1. (A) (B) (C)

   2. (A) (B) (C)

   3. (A) (B) (C)

   4. (A) (B) (C)

2 次のグラフに関する対話を聞き、それぞれの質問に対する適切な 選択肢を選びましょう。 CD 1-50

   1. What were Morinaga's annual sales when it started selling HI-CHEW in America?

     (A) $4 million

     (B) $40 million

     (C) $400 million

     (D) $4 billion

   2. How much were Morinaga's annual sales in 2017?

     (A) twice as much as in 2010

     (B) half of 2018

     (C) 10 times more than in 2010

     (D) three times as much as 2014

   3. What does Ms. Brown think is one of the reasons for the company's success?

     (A) giving a warm welcome

     (B) billions of marketing strategies

     (C) buying a sports team

     (D) supporting athletes

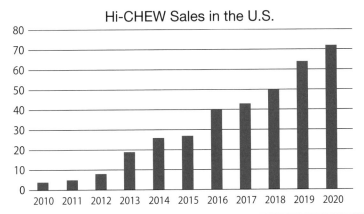

Hi-CHEW Sales in the U.S.

Year	2010	2011	2012	2013	2014	2015	2016	2017	2018	2019	2020
Sales (100million)	4	5	8	19	26	27	40	43	50	64	72

3 対話を聞き、それぞれの質問に対する適切な選択肢を選びましょう。 1-51

A

1. How many customers made a line on opening day at MUJI Vancouver?

   (A) 500　　(B) 1,000　　(C) 1,500　　(D) 5,000

2. Why is MUJI popular overseas?

   (A) Visitors can enjoy their hospitality.

   (B) The products lack Zen culture.

   (C) Small spaces and long lines are popular among local people.

   (D) Customers appreciate the simplicity of their product.

音声をもう一度聞き下の英文の（　　　　）に適切な表現を書き入れましょう。 1-52

B

A: MUJI is a popular brand overseas, including in the U.S. and Canada, isn't it?

B: Yes, indeed. When they opened a new store in Vancouver, Canada, more than 1,500 customers waited in a long line outside the store on opening day.

A: That's amazing. Why do their products [1](　　　　　　) so many local customers?

B: It is said that Western customers recognize the essence of Japanese Zen [2](　　　　　) in their simple products.

A: How is this done?

B: MUJI products create a sense of beauty by making the most of simple colors to highlight the shapes of [3](　　　　　) with fairly large spaces for product displays.

A: Ah, I see what you mean. When I visit their shops, I do feel relaxed and enjoy looking around at the simple displays.

B: The company also pays attention to minimizing their [4](　　　　　) impact and promotes recycling.

次はある本の広告です。下線部に入る最も適切な選択肢を選び英文を完成させましょう。

Focusing on Local: Kao Marketing in the U.S.A.

Editorial Reviews

This new book reveals the secret to the success of Kao USA's marketing strategies as illustrated in the following authentic business case:

• Kao introduced innovative skin care products to North America in 1997. It launched Bioré Pore Strips for nose pore cleansing. It became the top-selling ------- in the U.S.A.
1

• Its sales decreased because Kao USA adopted the global communication strategies requested by the headquarters.

• Kao USA reviewed the global strategies and changed ------- create
2

powerful advertising images for American consumers. Such localized communication strategies achieved great success.

• Bioré now uses this ------- communication strategy in more than 44
3
countries.

---

1. (A) hair color product

(B) body soap

(C) skin care product

(D) luxury cosmetics

3. (A) local

(B) Japanese-centered

(C) headquarters

(D) American-based

2. (A) for

(B) to

(C) with

(D) as

UNIT 2

Global Strategies

Using a New Guerrilla Marketing Strategy as a Challenger

Chapter 5

Coca-Cola in Laos

Coca-Cola uses cross-border supply chain strategies in the ASEAN countries.

　1886年に創業のザ コカ・コーラ カンパニーは、今や世界200か国以上で販売を行っている。2020年12月には売上高が330億1,400万ドルで営業利益は89億9,700万ドルとなっている。コカ・コーラとライバルのペプシ・コーラは、それぞれが優れたマーケティング戦略を展開し、世界各国において熾烈な売り上げ競争を行っている。

ラオスでは社会主義政権が長期にわたりペプシに独占販売権を与えていた。このため、1980年代初頭からコカ・コーラの販売は認められず、コーラ系飲料ではペプシが長期に渡って独占状態であった。ラオスのWTO加盟の予定もあり、2012年にようやくコカ・コーラの販売が認められた。だが、それまでほぼ100%のシェアを持っていたペプシのブランド力は強く、シェア拡大は容易でなかった。LCC（Laos Coca-Cola）は新規に参入した企業として、販売店の確保や物流の整備を最初から行わなければならなかった。

Warm-up

写真に関する英文を聞き学習の準備をしましょう。最も適切な選択肢を選びましょう。 1-53

(A)　　(B)　　(C)　　(D)

Vocabulary Input

次の英語に合う日本語を選び記号で答えましょう。 1-54

1. beverage　　　　　　　（　　）
2. price and quantity　　（　　）
3. tidy up　　　　　　　（　　）
4. monopoly　　　　　　（　　）
5. customs procedures　（　　）
6. production line　　　（　　）
7. distribution networks（　　）

(A) 独占　　　　　　(B) 製造ライン　　(C) 税関手続き　　(D) 片付ける

(E) 物流ネットワーク　(F) 清涼飲料水　　(G) 値段と量

Learning Important Expressions for Business Case Studies

ビジネスケースの理解に重要な表現に関連する下記の英文を完成させましょう。

1. The Laos market was ------- to change recently.

(A) in   (B) for   (C) about   (D) off

2. PepsiCo is the biggest ------- for the Coca-Cola Company.

(A) fighter   (B) companion   (C) monopoly   (D) competitor

3. They ------- with large grocery stores in the capital of Laos.

(A) commute   (B) cooperate   (C) corporate   (D) cofound

Listening Booster

LCC のビジネスケースに関する以下のグラフを参考にして質問に答えましょう。 1-55

A. Listen to the talk and choose the best answer to each question.

1. Why did LCC's share increase from 7.3 percent to 12.6 percent?

(A) Because it created a monopoly.

(B) Because it opened a new factory.

(C) Because it sold its shares.

(D) Because it became the market leader.

2. What year did Pepsi experience the greatest loss in market share?

(A) 2013   (B) 2015   (C) 2016   (D) 2017

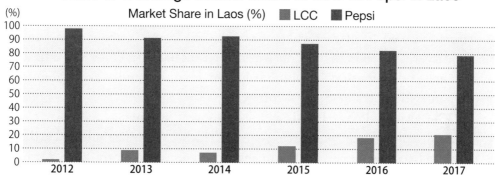

Table 1. Beverage Market Share of LCC vs Pepsi in Laos

Year	2012	2013	2014	2015	2016	2017
LCC	1.9	8.8	7.3	12.6	18.6	21.1
Pepsi	98.1	91.2	92.7	87.4	82.6	78.9

B. Listening Review

Ａの音声をもう一度聞き下の英文の（　　　）に適切な表現を書き入れましょう。 1-56

A: In order to break Pepsi's [1](　　　　), LCC developed various strategies and gradually increased its market share.

B: Could you show us the evidence?

A: Sure. Please look at Table 1. It shows the [2](　　　　) in market shares from 2012 to 2017. Most notable is that after the new factory opened in August 2015, LCC's market share increased remarkably in the [3](　　　) years.

B: I see. LCC has done a lot to grow its initially [4](　　　　) market share to over 21 percent within six years.

A: It can be said that the company's goal to become the [5](　　　　) leader in Laos has been steadily succeeding.

Learning From Authentic Business Examples

次のビジネスレポートを読んで以下の質問に答えましょう。 1-57〜59

Marketing Business Report

New Guerrilla Marketing

Pepsi had monopolized the soft drink market in Laos. To break the monopoly, Mr. Mark Griffin, the new CEO of LCC, introduced new guerrilla marketing. This strategy focuses on products and prices. For example, Pepsi sold its main products in ten-ounce glass bottles for 3000
5　kip (36 yen) and in 500 ml PET bottles for 5,000 kip (60 yen). However, LCC changed its products' sizes and made the prices cheaper. As seen in Table 2, LCC started selling some smaller amounts of cola at cheaper prices and larger sizes of cola at the same price as Pepsi's main products. This strategy aimed to attract customers who cared more about price and
10　quantity, rather than taste. This was successful because Pepsi had a fixed system for distributing its standard-sized products and was unable to compete with LCC's new size strategy.

To also challenge Pepsi on its sponsoring of music concerts, LCC decided to sponsor sporting events. This was significant because the
15　people of Laos love soccer. LCC launched a big campaign for the 2014 World Cup in Brazil. It started soccer clinics which helped young people improve their soccer skills. Moreover, members of Chelsea F.C. of the English Premier League were invited to interact with the Lao people.

LCC improved its domestic distribution networks and secured dealers to deal with poor road conditions. To increase the number of stores selling its drinks, LCC developed 250 new licensed outlets. In addition, the latest Coca-Cola refrigerators were installed in 1,000 local stores free of charge, which LCC employees frequently visited to tidy up the displays and put Coca-Cola products in the most prominent places.

	Pepsi		LCC		
	Size	Price (kip)	Size	Price (kip)	20
Bottle			6.5 oz	2,000	
	10 oz	3,000	15 oz	3,000	
			450 ml	4,000	
PET	500 ml	5,000	1 L	5,000	25
	1.25 L	8,000	1.5 L	8,000	
	2 L	11,000			
oz: ounce(s), ml: milliliter(s), L: liter(s)					

Table 2. Sizes and Prices of Pepsi vs. LCC in Laos

Notes

· **ten ounces : oz**（オンス）ビン入りコカ・コーラの標準サイズ 約 283.5 ml　· **kip**（キープ）ラオスの通貨
· **a fixed system** 固定したシステム
· **Chelsea F.C. of the English Premier League** 英国プレミアリーグの人気強豪チーム
· **the most prominent places** 最も目立つ場所

本文の内容として正しい場合は T を、正しくない場合は F を（　）に書きましょう。

1. LCC changed its products' sizes and made the prices cheaper. 　　　（　　）

2. According to Table 2, Pepsi's 2L PET is the same price as LCC's 2.5L PET. 　（　　）

3. The company put Coca-Cola products in the most prominent places. 　（　　）

▶ **Reading Booster**

次の LCC のビジネスケースを読んで質問に答えましょう。　 1-60,61

Cross-border Supply Chain Strategy

　　LCC did not have a production plant like Pepsi in Laos and relied on importing products from Thailand. However, the customs procedures at the Laos border were complicated, time-consuming, and frequently delayed. As a result, the lead time from product ordering to delivery and sales became longer, and transportation costs increased. Moreover, a new domestic factory seemed unable to solve this problem because the Laos market is small and constructing a new factory would be an overinvestment.

To solve such problems, LCC set up a cross-border supply chain strategy. The purpose was to make Laos a major manufacturing base by taking advantage of tax exemptions in this country within the ASEAN economy. Moreover, Laos has a lot of
10 benefits, such as cheap electricity, low labor costs, and abundant water for manufacturing beverages. In 2015, LCC opened a new factory in the north of Vientiane at a cost of $30 million. With the cooperation of the Laos government, they constructed a highway from Vientiane to the factory. There are three large production lines in this factory, even though one production line is enough for the Laos market. The remaining two lines are
15 production lines for northern Thailand, where soft-drink consumption has increased. The construction of this factory not only improved distribution in Laos, but it was also part of a cross-border supply chain strategy that links LCC with all of the ASEAN countries.

Notes

· **a production plant** 生産工場　· **lead time** リードタイム（所要時間）
· **a cross-border supply chain** 国境を越えた供給網
· **the ASEAN economy** アセアン経済圏：圏内の関税を互いに免除している
· **Vientiane** ラオスの首都ビエンチャン

1. What is one of the differences between LCC and Pepsi in Laos?

(A) Pepsi had customs trouble.

(B) Pepsi no longer gets products to customers.

(C) Pepsi did not have a production plant.

(D) Pepsi did not have to import products.

2. Why did LCC NOT want to open a domestic factory in Laos?

(A) Because the transportation costs would be too high.

(B) Because it would cost too much money.

(C) Because sales would be too great.

(D) Because it would delay product deliveries.

3. How did LCC benefit from a cross-border supply chain strategy?

(A) They did not have to pay so much money in taxes.

(B) They were able to use two production lines for Laos.

(C) They were able to send water from Laos to Thailand.

(D) They linked ASEAN countries with Europe.

Mr. James Quincey,
The Coca-Cola Company CEO

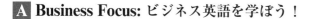

A Business Focus: ビジネス英語を学ぼう！

New Guerrilla Marketing Strategy ネオ・ゲリラマーケティング戦略
ゲリラマーケティングは、一般に新規参入企業などが、市場で優位な地位を築いている大企業のシェアを奪うため、大手ができない小回りの利いた、奇抜なアイディアを実行するマーケティング。問題点として、短期的には顧客の注目を集めるが、効果が一過性である。この弱点を補うため、先行企業が困難な戦略を一定の資金を投入して、他の様々な効果的な戦略と並行して継続して推進する戦略。

Cross-border Supply Chain Strategy
１つの国で解決できない工場建設の問題を、ASEAN 全体の市場を攻める戦略の手段の一つとして、製品の供給拠点として活用することで実現している。

B ビジネス英語の理解を深めよう！

Guerrilla marketing に関する以下の例文を与えられた文字に続くように空所をうめて完成させましょう。この際、本文を再度確認し、関連する他の事象にも下線を引き C のタスクにも活用できるようにしましょう。

1. LCC started selling some (s   ) amounts of cola at (c   ) prices and
(l   ) sizes of cola at the (s   ) price as Pepsi's main products.

2. Pepsi had a fixed system for (d   ) their standard-sized products and were
unable to (c   ) with LCC's new (s   ) strategy.

3. LCC decided to sponsor (s   ) events for the 2014 World (C   ) in
Brazil because Lao People (l   ) football.

4. To increase the (n   ) of stores (s   ) its drinks, LCC developed 250
new (l   ) outlets.

C Business Discussion

Bの表現を参考にして、次のテーマについてクラスメートと話し合いましょう。

What are examples of new guerrilla marketing?

- _____

  _____

  _____

- _____

  _____

  _____

- _____

  _____

  _____

- _____

  _____

  _____

Countering Innovator's Dilemma

Toshiba Vietnam

Toshiba has been famous for inventing new technologies.

　東芝は日本を代表する大手電機メーカーで、日本製のテレビや冷蔵庫を発明した。現在は、消費者向け製品からは撤退した。しかし、これまで世界初のラップトップ型コンピューター Dynabook や、優れた半導体技術を活用した液晶テレビ Regza などを製品化してきた。家電製品は、今や後発の韓国や中国企業が日本企業の技術を模倣し、低価格で販売し、優れたマーケティング力でアジアなどの市場を占有していった。これは、不利な状況で東芝ベトナムがテレビ事業で成功したビジネスケースである。

2000年まで日本の家電産業は世界のテレビの50%以上を生産していた。しかし、2005年には30%になり次第にシェアを落としていく。この背景には、韓国や中国などの家電メーカーが、品質は悪くても価格などがかなり安い製品を新興国に販売し始めたことがある。最初は粗悪な品質でも、次第に現地に適合した製品を製造し支持を得て行った。また、先行している日本企業が開発した技術をまねることで、それほど開発費もかからずに品質を向上できた。結果として、高品質を訴求し続け、価格も高い日本製品は急激にシェアを落とした。これはベトナムでも同じ状況で、現地の東芝家電事業は事態打開のための新たな戦略が必要であった。

Warm-up

写真に関する英文を聞き学習の準備をしましょう。最も適切な選択肢を選びましょう。　 1-62

(A)　　(B)　　(C)　　(D)

Vocabulary Input

次の英語に合う日本語を選び記号で答えましょう。　🎧 1-63

1. corporate report　　　（　　）

2. cutting-edge　　　（　　）

3. strict quality standards　　　（　　）

4. breakdowns　　　（　　）

5. after-sales service　　　（　　）

6. latecomers　　　（　　）

7. home appliances　　　（　　）

(A) アフターサービス	(B) 企業情報誌	(C) 故障	(D) 最先端の
(E) 家電製品	(F) 厳格な品質基準	(G) 後期参入者	

ビジネスケースの理解に重要な表現に関連する下記の英文を完成させましょう。

1. Despite ------- to a Chinese company, that TV brand is very popular.

(A) they have licenced   (B) it was licensing   (C) to be licensed

(D) being licensed

2. There was a demand for cheap televisions ------- matched lower incomes.

(A) what   (B) that   (C) there   (D) where

3. These foreign latecomers could ------- Japanese products easily.

(A) invent   (B) implement   (C) imitate   (D) initiate

► **Listening Booster** ▌▌▌

企業情報に関する英文を聞いて背景を理解しましょう。 1-64

A. Listen and choose the best answer to each question.

1. What product is Toshiba NOT credited with inventing in Japan?

(A) the TV   (B) the dryer   (C) the refrigerator   (D) the washing machine

2. When did Toshiba let a Chinese company sell its products?

(A) 1950   (B) 1983   (C) 2018   (D) 2020

B. Listening Review

Aの音声をもう一度聞き下の英文の（　　　　）に適切な表現を書き入れましょう。 1-65

Toshiba is famous for inventing the first TV, refrigerator, and washing machine in Japan. In fact, Toshiba has always been famous for inventing [1]( ) technologies and building high-quality products. Especially, the Regza brand of TVs are famous around the world, despite being licensed to a Chinese company in 2018. In Vietnam, the TV brand and other consumer [2]( ) made by Toshiba have been gaining in popularity since 1993. At first, however, only a few products were sold in Vietnam, but as soon as the Vietnamese learned of the brand's reliability, sales [3]( ). Toshiba's popularity, not only in Vietnam and Japan but also around the world, can be seen in the company's [4]( ) report. In 2020, Toshiba's net sales were 3.3 trillion yen, and the total number of employees was 125,648. In addition, Toshiba had more than 50 overseas subsidiaries and affiliated companies.

Notes

· **Regza** 東芝が開発したテレビブランド　　· **affiliated companies** 関連会社

> ## Learning From Authentic Business Examples ▌▌▌

次のビジネス雑誌の記事を読んで以下の質問に答えましょう。　　🎧 CD 1-66,67

Business Review

Suffering From Innovator's Dilemma

In emerging countries, there was a demand for cheap televisions that matched lower incomes. Such low-priced models were not profitable for Japanese companies, which produced consumer electronics according to strict quality standards. When Korean companies started doing business in emerging countries,
5　like Vietnam, they focused their sales on low-income families by selling low-priced TVs. These products were suitable for local consumers and sales increased rapidly. This is called a disruptive technology. In the beginning, however, Korean televisions had many problems because of poor build quality. As a result, Korean companies needed to establish many local service centers to provide customer support for
10　breakdowns and after-sales service. The frequent visits to these centers by local customers gave Korean companies the opportunity to talk with customers and learn of their preferences. This meant that they could conduct effective marketing communication for local needs.

As these latecomers were able to imitate Japanese products, they could save
15　their profits for the research and development of new technologies. As a result, Korean companies were able to sell products that were both inexpensive and more advanced than Japanese companies. Samsung, for example, had entered the lower-level markets of emerging countries and had successfully developed products that the majority of local consumers wanted. Thus, its sales increased, and it developed
20　brand power. In Vietnam, for example, it expanded its market share, while Toshiba's TV sales decreased to only 5.9 percent in 2009, and Toshiba became trapped in the Innovator's Dilemma.

Notes

· **innovator's dilemma** イノベーターのジレンマ　　· **consumer electronics** 家電製品
· **disruptive technology** 破壊的技術　　· **Samsung** 韓国を代表する企業サムソン

本文の内容として正しい場合は T を、正しくない場合は F を（　）に書きましょう。

1. Consumers in developing countries preferred to buy products that were made under strict quality standards. (　)

2. Korean companies learned consumers' preferences and adapted to local needs. (　)

3. Samsung's success is due to the fact that it spent a lot of money on research and development. (　)

東芝ベトナムのビジネスケースを読んで質問に答えましょう。 1-68〜71

Countering Innovator's Dilemma

　　　To stop the decline in sales, Toshiba set up and implemented effective strategies for the marketing mix in 2009. For the product strategy, it combined different technologies at Toshiba TV Division to make "Power TVs." These TVs are equipped with a lithium-ion battery which lasts up to two hours after a power outage. This is important in emerging countries because of unstable power and frequent power outages. Also, the 5 TVs have a receiver called a power booster, which can strengthen radio waves so that people can have clearer images on their TVs, even in remote areas. Moreover, because many Vietnamese watch TV in large family groups, they prefer louder volumes. The Power TVs have two 10W speakers, which allows people to enjoy louder volumes.

　　　Toshiba set the price for 21-inch Power TVs at 40,000 dong (about 18,000 yen), 10 which is twice the price of the best-selling competitor's product. This is a price premium strategy that stimulates purchasing motivation by proposing prices with advanced technologies that are believed to be valuable.

　　　For the place strategy, Toshiba Vietnam increased the number of sales outlets

15 from 400 stores to 1,096. This was done by introducing "a mini road show kit." This kit allowed Toshiba Vietnam to sell its products in a small area of a store. Moreover, it increased the number of affiliated service centers to 81. This gave its customers more access to repair centers and places where they could go to ask questions about products. For the promotion strategy, Toshiba Vietnam used a famous Vietnamese actress to
20 promote the Toshiba brand.

Thanks to these marketing mix strategies, Toshiba's sales increased, and it gained the largest market share of 28.6 percent in September 2011. Simultaneously, Toshiba's brand power improved, and the total sales of home appliances increased to 15.3 billion yen in 2012, which is more than 10 times larger than it was in 2008.

Notes

· **TV Division** テレビ事業部　· **a lithium-ion battery** リチウムイオン電池　· **power outage** 停電
· **receiver** 受信機　· **power booster** パワーブースターと呼ばれる受信装置
· **radio wave** 電波　· **10W speakers** 10 ワットのスピーカー。通常のテレビは３ワットから６ワット
· **dong** ベトナムの通貨ドン　· **a mini road show kit** 狭い場所に置ける製品と梱包の箱を並べた稼働式の棚

1. What makes Toshiba's Power TV so unique?

(A) It was made before 2009.

(B) It was made for developed countries.

(C) It was made with cheap parts.

(D) It was made to work during a power outage.

2. According to the reading, what is a price premium strategy?

(A) A way to make consumers think a cheap product is expensive.

(B) A way of getting celebrities to promote a product.

(C) A way of promoting advanced technologies at an expensive price.

(D) A sales strategy that the Vietnamese created.

3. What was a benefit of the place strategy?

(A) It used the biggest area in a store to call attention to Toshiba's products.

(B) It resulted in greater access to Toshiba's products.

(C) It allowed Toshiba to discount their Power TVs.

(D) It allowed Toshiba to use cars to promote their TVs.

A Business Focus: ビジネス英語を学ぼう！

Innovator's Dilemma イノベーターのジレンマ
クリステンセン教授が 1997 年に提唱した理論。優良大企業が、顧客により良いサービスの提供に邁進することで、競争力を失う理由を説明した経営理論。大企業が取り組めないような、新興企業の安価で質の良くない破壊的技術が、やがて消費者の支持を拡大し、品質も改善され、市場を奪ってしまう状況を指摘した。

Destructive Technology in Home Appliances 家電製品の破壊的技術
韓国や中国の家電メーカーは、当初は質の悪い製品で新興国などに参入した。値段が安いため収入の低い層に売れた。頻繁に故障するため、修理するセンターをたくさん作る必要があった。頻繁に訪れる顧客の苦情や要望に応えることによって、次第に現地に適合する製品を作るようになった。先行している日本企業の技術をまねることで研究開発にかける予算も削減できた。結果として品質も改善でき、現地の消費者に、より適合した製品を提供し、市場を占有していった。

B ビジネス英語の理解を深めよう！

東芝ベトナムが行ったイノベーターのジレンマへの対抗に関する以下の例文を、与えられた文字に続くように空所をうめて完成させましょう。この際、本文を再度確認し、関連する他の事象にも下線を引き C のタスクにも活用できるようにしましょう。

1. Toshiba (p   ) a Power TV (e   ) with a lithium-ion battery which lasts up to two hours after a power (o   ).

2. It introduced a price (p   ) strategy that used (a   ) technology to stimulate a desire to buy by making people believe that the technology is (v   ).

3. Toshiba Vietnam (i   ) the number of sales (o   ) from 400 (s   ) to 1,096.

4. It used a (f   ) Vietnamese actress to (p   ) the Toshiba brand to (l   ) consumers.

C Business Discussion

B の表現を参考にして、次のテーマについてクラスメートと話し合いましょう。

What are some ways to counter innovator's dilemma?

1. Product

   _____

   _____

2. Price

   _____

   _____

3. Place

   _____

   _____

4. Promotion

   _____

   _____

Honda Motor has expanded its business to other countries because of the accelerated development of cutting-edge technology.

　本田技研工業は世界最大のエンジンメーカーとしてオートバイ・自動車や航空機などを製造販売している。世界で 430 のグループ企業を持ち、従業員の総数は 21 万 8 千人以上である。独自の高い技術力で、排気ガスを画期的に削減した自動車の CVCC エンジンや、2 足歩行型ロボット ASIMO、小型ビジネスジェット機 HondaJet なども開発してきた。大企業になるにつれ、社内の連携や効果的なコミュニケーション活動が重要になってきた。今や世界 72 か国でビジネスを行っている。2020 年度の売上高は 13,820 億円で、営業利益は 1,756 億円を記録している。

企業の規模が大きくなると、社内コミュニケーションがうまくいかなくなる。結果として、意思決定が遅れたり、創造的な技術革新が停滞したりする。卓越した技術力を誇り、先進的な取組みをしてきた本田技研工業は、このような中でも可能な限り若手にも機会を与え、新たなイノベーションを目指している。特に将来を見据えた電気自動車などの開発を推進するには、さらなる挑戦に取り組む必要があった。

▶ **Warm-up**

写真に関する英文を聞き学習の準備をしましょう。最も適切な選択肢を選びましょう。　CD 1-72

(A)　　(B)　　(C)　　(D)

▶ **Vocabulary Input**

次の英語に合う日本語を選び記号で答えましょう。 CD 1-73

1. strong resistance 　　　（　　）
2. come up with 　　　（　　）
3. stakeholders 　　　（　　）
4. potential core buyers 　　　（　　）
5. electric vehicle 　　　（　　）
6. customer value 　　　（　　）

(A) 潜在的な主要購入者	(B) 利害関係者	(C) 顧客の価値
(D) 強い抵抗	(E) 思いつく	(F) 電気自動車

ビジネスケースの理解に重要な表現に関連する下記の英文を完成させなさい。

1. The manager was put in ------- of luxury car sales.

   (A) spite   (B) charge   (C) order   (D) sake

2. Matsuda suggested ------- this equipment from the RDX.

   (A) remove   (B) to remove   (C) to be removed   (D) removing

3. That idea was very effective; ------- his project was not appreciated.

   (A) however   (B) and   (C) then   (D) so

Listening Booster

企業情報に関する年表を読み、英文を聞いて背景を理解しましょう。 1-74

A. Listen to the conversation about the following chart and choose the best answer to each question.

Brief History of the Case

1982	Manufacturing automobiles in the U.S.
1986	Launching Acura in the U.S.
1997	EV cars
2013	Acura RDX
2015	HondaJet
2020	Honda e

1. Which country did they mention?

   (A) Japan   (B) Canada   (C) Korea   (D) China

2. How did the woman describe the Honda EV car?

   (A) as a surprising product   (B) as an innovative technology

   (C) as a challenging strategy   (D) as brand-new

3. Which year's event in the table was NOT mentioned in their talk?

   (A) 1997   (B) 2013   (C) 2015   (D) 2020

B. Listening Review

Ａの音声をもう一度聞き下の英文の（　）に適切な表現を書き入れましょう。 1-75

A: Shall we review the Honda business case study?

B: Sure. Honda started producing[1](   ) in 1964. In 1982, it became the first Japanese company to start manufacturing automobiles in the U.S.

A: That's right. Then in 1986 it launched the first Japanese [2](   ) car, the Acura RDX, in the U.S.

B: It was very ambitious to be the first company to start a new project overseas.

A: It's [3](   ), isn't it? In 2013, 35,000 Acura RDX were sold in the U.S.

B: I was surprised that the company had already produced EV cars in 1997.

A: It's very [4](   ). However, its first EV car did not work well.

B: But, in 2020, it launched the brand-new EV called Honda e, which won the Car of the Year Award in Germany.

Learning From Authentic Business Examples

ホンダのビジネスケースに関する英文を読んで後の問いに答えましょう。 1-76

Business Case Study Series

In 2007, Mr. Toshifumi Matsuda was put in charge of the Acura SUV (sport utility vehicle) planning team to improve the brand image and sales. Initially, Matsuda carefully investigated the market and frequently communicated with the American sales team. His efforts revealed that the potential core buyers
5 were women in their 30s, rather than men in their 20s. These consumers wanted less expensive SUVs. Moreover, they preferred quiet SUVs that had more interior space, rather than ones that went fast. To meet these needs, a new RDX needed to have some options removed. Matsuda doubted the necessity of expensive, superior-handling equipment, which is a core technology of the
10 Acura lines. This enables drivers to corner at speeds as high as 100 km/h. To reduce the cost, Matsuda suggested removing this equipment from the RDX, but this recommendation faced strong resistance from the engineers on the team. However, Matsuda never gave up and kept explaining about customer value. This was effective at getting him support from the engineers one by one. Moreover,
15 he received strong support from the American sales staff and executives. After many negotiations with all the stakeholders, he was able to convince upper management of his idea. In 2013, the Acura RDX successfully launched in the American market, recording sales of 35,000 cars, which was more than double the 13,000 annual sales of the previous model. These results show that Honda
20 respects active participation and discussions rather than relying on company hierarchy to solve problems.

Notes

· **superior-handlining** 100 キロの高速でもスムーズにカーブを回ることが可能になる装備
· **Acura RDX** ホンダが日本企業で最初に米国で立ち上げた高級自動車ブランドのアキュラの SUV 車種
· **hierarchy** 序列

本文の内容として正しい場合は T を、正しくない場合は F を（　）に書きましょう。

1. The American potential core buyers of SUVs were women in their 20s. （　　）

2. Matsuda suggested removing superior-handling equipment from the RDX. （　　）

3. By getting the help of American local staff, the Acura RDX recorded sales of 13,000 cars in 2013. （　　）

> **Reading Booster**

次の Honda のビジネスケースを読んで内容を理解しましょう。   1-77〜79

Revising Electric Vehicles for Sustainable Development

To create a future business model, Honda planned a new project. The current problem is that the younger generation in urban areas is less interested in cars because of high costs, including urban parking fees. Matsuda was moved to the business strategy department and critically examined the current automobile business. He came up with an electric vehicle (EV) business model like the mobile phone business model. That is, 5 customers would pay a certain monthly usage fee to drive a car that would become their own after several years. To realize his vision, Matsuda proposed a smaller electric car with two seats that would be sold for less than 500 thousand yen. In addition, this car has an elongated body, so two of these cars can be placed in one residential parking space. The owner of the cars can use one space to take advantage of a car sharing 10

61

business with neighbors to earn some pocket money.

Matsuda proposed the idea at a Honda new business contest. Many judges favored his unique proposal, but it was not accepted because of safety concerns. Matsuda never gave up and kept exploring the possibility for an EV business. He
15 gradually expanded his network and found that Honda had once produced EV cars in 1997, an initiative that had failed. The chief engineer of the original project continued working on EV systems, but his project was not appreciated. Matsuda, however, instantly knew how valuable he was, so he persuaded the engineer to explain the superiority of the latest EV technology in front of the company's decision makers. This was a success
20 and enabled them to restart EV projects.

Recently, Honda engineers have made great efforts to develop effective EVs. In 2020, Honda launched the brand-new EV called Honda e, which won the Car of the Year Award in Germany. Subsequently, Matsuda organized and set up the e:Technology brand to accelerate Honda's EV Strategy.

Notes

· **elongated body** 細長い車体　　· **residential parking space** 自宅の駐車場
· **Honda e** 2020 年ヨーロッパ、日本で販売開始した Honda の電気自動車
· **Car of the Year Award** その年の最も優れた自動車に贈られる賞

1. Why did Honda create a new project?

(A) Because it was not selling many cars to younger people.

(B) Because older people did not like the Honda brand.

(C) Because urban parking lots were so popular.

(D) Because customers would not agree to pay monthly fees.

2. What is NOT a feature of Matsuda's electric vehicle?

(A) It can only fit two people.

(B) It is short and wide.

(C) It costs under 500,000 yen.

(D) It can fit in half of a parking space.

3. Why did the executives at Honda agree to the Honda e project?

(A) Because they knew they could win the Car of the Year Award.

(B) Because they had safety concerns.

(C) Because they realized the benefits of the latest EV technology.

(D) Because they did not want to meet any more engineers.

A Business Focus: ビジネス英語を学ぼう！

Engineer-driven Company
Honda R&D Co. Ltd. has been playing a significant role in developing new technologies and cutting-edge products.
ホンダは技術者が中心となる企業で、その中心が（株）本田技術研究所であり、ここから様々な先進的な技術を生み出した。歴代の CEO のほとんどがここの出身者である。

Enhancing communication against big company disease
組織が大きくなると階層や部門でのコミュニケーションが困難になりがちである。この中でホンダでは、従業員同士の自由な議論や積極的な参加を尊重し、顧客に役立つ新たな技術や製品を生み出してきた。

B ビジネス英語の理解を深めよう！

Honda のケースに関する以下の例文を与えられた文字に続くように空所をうめて完成させましょう。この際、本文を再度確認し、関連する他の事象にも下線を引き C のタスクにも活用できるようにしましょう。

1. His mission was to improve the (*b*   ) image and sales of RDX, but he (*f*   ) strong (*r*   ) from engineers to his proposal.

2. He conducted many (*n*   ) with all the (*s*   ), and he was able to convince upper management of his idea.

3. He proposed a (*s*   ) electric car with (*t*   ) seats, but it was not (*a*   ) because of (*s*   ) concerns.

4. He (*p*   ) the chief engineer to (*e*   ) the superiority of the latest EV (*t*   ) in front of the company's (*d*   ) makers.

Business Discussion

の表現を参考にして、次のテーマについてクラスメートと話し合いましょう。

How did Mr. Matsuda develop communication strategies in the following projects?

• Acura RDX

1. What was his mission?

_____

_____

2. What were the problems?

_____

_____

3. How did he solve the problems?

_____

_____

• EV project

1. What kind of a business model did he propose?

_____

_____

2. What were the problems?

_____

_____

3. How did he solve the problems?

_____

_____

Focus Strategy and Cost Leadership Strategy in Frozen Food Industry

Hatchando Vietnam

いつも、おいしく。
もっと、おいしく。

Focusing on Innovative Food Business

　川邊義隆は 1976 年、たこ焼きの日本のファーストフード化を目指し福岡県に(株)八ちゃん堂を開業した。1985 年に冷凍たこ焼きを開発しヒット商品となり、生産量は 1 日 100 万個を超えた。1996 年に冷凍焼きなすを開発したが、日本での生産では採算が合わない。このため海外での製造を目指しベトナムに進出することを決めた。そして現在、同社の海外戦略は成功している。2020 年には、冷凍たこ焼き事業も一層拡大し、年間 2,000 トン以上を生産している。

Business Issue ベトナムにおける農業の企業化

　福岡に本社のある八ちゃん堂は冷凍たこ焼を日本で最初に製造し成功を収めた。しかし、この市場に大手企業が参入し、次第に競争が厳しくなってきた。社長の川邊は、次なる経営の柱として冷凍焼きナスを販売することを考えついた。製造販売を始めたが、福岡は記録的な渇水となりナスの価格が高騰し、国内生産は一層困難になった。ベトナムで製品を作る計画を立て進出したが、様々な問題に直面して生産は進まなかった。

Warm-up

写真に関する英文を聞き学習の準備をしましょう。最も適切な選択肢を選びましょう。　🎧 1-80

(A)　　(B)　　(C)　　(D)

Vocabulary Input

次の英語に合う日本語を選び記号で答えましょう。　🎧 1-81

1. franchise chain　　　　　(　　　)
2. mobile sales vehicles　　(　　　)
3. frozen *takoyaki*　　　　(　　　)
4. frozen roasted eggplant　(　　　)
5. baking and peeling　　　(　　　)
6. management resources　　(　　　)
7. labor cost　　　　　　　(　　　)

(A) 冷凍焼きナス　　(B) 労務費　　　(C) フランチャイズ　　(D) 経営資源

(E) 移動販売車　　　(F) 冷凍たこ焼き　(G) 焼いて皮をはぐ

ビジネスケースの理解に重要な表現に関連する下記の英文を完成させましょう。

1. ------- of franchise stores expanded to 300 in the 1980s.

    (A) A number   (B) Most   (C) The number   (D) The most

2. Production at this price would be in the -------.

    (A) ocean   (B) red   (C) dark   (D) bright

3. Finally, they gave up on ------- and built their own factory.

    (A) outcoming   (B) outgoing   (C) outstanding   (D) outsourcing

Listening Booster

企業情報に関する英文を聞いて背景を理解しましょう。 CD 1-82

A. Listen and choose the best answer to each question.

1. What was Mr. Kawabe's aim in 1976?

    (A) He wanted to create a *takoyaki* fast food chain.

    (B) He wanted to farm *takoyaki*.

    (C) He wanted to drive mobile sales vehicles.

    (D) He wanted to eat *takoyaki* in cars.

2. What is Hatchando's second biggest hit product?

    (A) *takoyaki*   (B) a fast food franchise chain

    (C) octopus dumplings   (D) frozen roasted eggplant

B. Listening Review

A の音声をもう一度聞き下の英文の (　　　　) に適切な表現を書き入れましょう。 CD 1-83

Brief History of Hatchando

Year	Events
1976	Hatchando Co., Ltd. set up with the aim of making *takoyaki* a Japanese fast food franchise chain.
1980's	There were [1](　　　　　) mobile sales vehicles. The number of franchise stores expanded to [2](　　　　).
[3](　　　)	Developing frozen *takoyaki*. Producing more than 1 million pieces a day.
[4](　　　)	Developing frozen roasted eggplant.
2020	The group company's annual sales totaled [5](　　　　　) yen.

八ちゃん堂のビジネスケースに関する英字新聞記事を読んで後の問いに答えましょう。 1-84～86

Utilizing Focus Strategy and Cost Leadership Strategy in the Frozen Food Market

Once Hatchando established the initial frozen *takoyaki* market, many competitors, including big frozen food companies, entered the market. To compete with their prices, Hatchando developed the world's largest frozen *takoyaki* machine that could produce 20,000 *takoyaki* per hour. It used its management resources to focus on this product.

Setakamachi, where the Hatchando factory is located, is a very famous production area for Japanese eggplant. Thus, Kawabe decided to produce frozen roasted eggplant that could be used simply by thawing it without the hassle of baking and peeling it. The hope was that it would be in demand as a buffet ingredient for major hotels and restaurants.

Hatchando initially planned to set the price for the frozen roasted eggplant at 1,500 yen per kilogram because the estimated cost was 1,300 yen. However, the salespeople from the company's wholesaler suggested that the price should be around 800 yen per kilogram. Even though production at this price would be in the red, Kawabe decided on a cost leadership strategy and sold the eggplant for 700 yen per kilogram. He did this because no other companies were producing such products, and this meant that there would be a huge demand. Additionally, by producing it overseas, they could reduce the cost and monopolize the market before other companies entered the market. Ultimately, Hatchando moved production overseas to Vietnam in 1996, and this stopped the early losses resulting from production in Japan.

Notes

· **focus strategy** 集中戦略 · **thawing** 解凍 · **buffet ingredient** ビュッフェの食材
· **per kilogram** 1 キロ当たり · **company's wholesaler** 会社の問屋業者 · **monopolize** 独占する

本文の内容として正しい場合はTを、正しくない場合はFを（　　）に書きましょう。

1. *Takoyaki* machines could produce 20,000 *takoyaki* per day.　　　　　　（　　）

2. Kawabe expected that the frozen roasted eggplant would be in demand as a buffet
   ingredient for large hotels and restaurants.　　　　　　（　　）

3. After moving production overseas, Hatchando could stop the early losses that were
   the result of production in Vietnam.　　　　　　（　　）

> **Reading Booster**

八ちゃん堂のビジネスケースを読んで内容を理解しましょう。　　　　　　1-87〜91

Producing Frozen Roasted Eggplant in Vietnam

　　　In Vietnam, the weather is ideal for growing eggplant, and labor costs are low. Initially, Hatchando tried to outsource the process of farming and freezing eggplant. However, it faced slow and complex behavior from local contractors. In the end, it gave up on outsourcing and built its own factory and farm in the Tan Thanh export processing zone in Ho Chi Minh City. In June 1996, it established a wholly owned subsidiary, 5 Hatchando Vietnam, with 300 local employees and obtained 400,000 square meters of farmland to start growing eggplant.

　　　Building its own factory was not without problems. To save on factory construction costs, Hatchando used a local construction company, who offered to build the factory for 800,000 US dollars, which was one-third of the price that the Japanese 10 contractors quoted. However, because the local company's planning was always delayed and construction specifications needed many revisions, the final costs for the factory ended up being much higher.

　　　There were various barriers to creating a global business in Vietnam. For

15 example, when importing refrigeration equipment, approval was required from the police, customs, and the Agriculture Quarantine Department. Moreover, these approvals always required bribes so that procedures went smoothly. Additionally, Hatchando found that some of its local managers were corrupt and needed to be dismissed.

20 Although Hatchando had to solve several problems, it gradually developed an effective business model. That is, it could realize cost reductions beyond their initial expectations: less than one-sixth of the cost to produce frozen roasted eggplant in Japan.

In 1996, the company's annual sales were 1 billion yen, but by 2005, sales grew to 2.5 billion yen. In 2020, it expanded its operations and produced more than 2,000 tons of frozen roasted eggplant. Furthermore, Hatchando started building a second 25 factory. Due to this success, the company group achieved more than five billion yen in annual sales in 2020.

Notes
· **local contractor** 地元の建築会社　·**Agriculture Quarantine Department** 農業検疫部
· **bribes** わいろ　·**corrupt** 汚職をしている

1. Why did Hatchando move frozen roasted eggplant production to Vietnam?

(A) Because the police were beneficial to the company.

(B) Because the weather is good, and wages are cheap.

(C) Because bribes were important to the company.

(D) Because Ho Chi Minh City is a good import zone.

2. What is NOT one of the difficulties that Hatchando faced in Vietnam?

(A) corrupt managers

(B) customs difficulties

(C) subsidized construction costs

(D) lengthy approval times

3. How much did Hatchando increase its annual sales from 2005 to 2020?

(A) 1 billion yen

(B) 1.5 billion yen

(C) 2.5 billion yen

(D) 4 billion yen

Tasks for Business Studies

A Business Focus: ビジネス英語を学ぼう！

Strategy for competitive advantage 競争優位のための戦略

According to Prof. Michael Porter, companies should develop a competitive advantage for creating and sustaining superior performance. They can introduce some effective strategies, such as Focus Strategy and Cost Leadership Strategy.
企業戦略研究者マイケル・ポーターは競争優位を確立するために集中戦略やコストリーダーシップ戦略の有効性を説いた。

Focus Strategy 集中戦略

The company can develop a competitive advantage by focusing on a specialized product in a niche market.
企業は特定の製品をニッチマーケットに集中させることで競争優位の確立が可能となる。

Cost Leadership Strategy コストリーダーシップ戦略

The company can increase market share by charging lower prices with innovative strategies.
革新的な戦略で低価格を実現すれば市場シェアの拡大が可能である。

B ビジネス英語の理解を深めよう！

競争優位のための戦略に関する以下の例文を、与えられた文字に続くように空所をうめて完成させましょう。この際、本文を再度確認し、関連する他の事象にも下線を引き C のタスクにも活用できるようにしましょう。

1. Hatchando (e   ) the (i   ) frozen *takoyaki* market before many competitors (e   ) the market.

2. Hatchando used management (r   ) to focus on developing the world's largest frozen *takoyaki* (m   ) that could (p   ) 20,000 *takoyaki* per hour.

3. Kawabe decided to produce frozen (r   ) eggplant because the company is in a very famous (p   ) area for Japanese (e   ).

4. By producing frozen roasted eggplant in (v), it could realize cost (r) beyond its initial (e).

C Business Discussion

B の表現を参考にして、次のテーマについてクラスメートと話し合いましょう。

What kind of strategies did Hatchando introduce in its business?

1. *Takoyaki*

Focus Strategy

_____

Cost Leadership

_____

2. Roasted eggplant

Focus Strategy

_____

Cost Leadership

_____

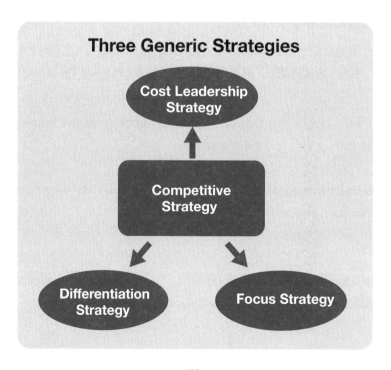

Three Generic Strategies

Cost Leadership Strategy

Competitive Strategy

Differentiation Strategy

Focus Strategy

Review Unit 2
Chapter5−8 の復習をしましょう

1 最も適切な応答の選択肢を選びましょう。　　🔘 1-92〜95

Listen to the question or statement and three responses. Then choose the best answer

1. (A) (B) (C)   **3.** (A) (B) (C)

2. (A) (B) (C)   **4.** (A) (B) (C)

2 本文を参考に以下のビジネスメールを完成させましょう。

与えられた文字に続くように空所をうめましょう。

E-mail

Dear Ms. May

I am writing with regard to your inquiry about Toshiba's success in Vietnam. After investigating the local market for two months, we have found out about their effective localization strategies.

This company set up and implemented effective strategies for the ¹(*m*　　　) (*m*　　　). For the product, they combined different technologies such as a lithium-ion battery and a power booster in order to adapt to local ²(*c*　　　) (*n*　　　). To enhance the place strategy, Toshiba Vietnam increased the number of ³(*s*　　　) (*o*　　　) to more than double. However, it did not sell the products at a low price. Instead, it used a ⁴(*p*　　　) (*p*　　　) strategy to create brand value.

If you need further information, we are able to provide you with detailed business reports about this case.

We are very much ⁵(*l*　　　) (*f*　　　) to working with you soon.

Sincerely yours,

Thomas Halliday

3 ビジネスケースを復習しよう！

以下の下線部に入る最も適切な選択肢を選び英文を完成させましょう。

Long History in Business

Honda Motor Co., Ltd was set up in 1948 and has been the world's largest motorcycle manufacturer since 1959. In 1964, it started producing automobiles and became famous for inventing an innovative engine which would drastically reduce toxic ------- by 1972. Additionally, in 1982, Honda
1

became the first Japanese company to manufacture automobiles in the U.S. Following this, it began expanding its business to other countries with the accelerated development of ------- technology. Furthermore, Honda created
2

the humanoid ------- ASIMO in 2000, and it launched HondaJet, a light
3

business jet, in 2015. Lastly, it has about 430 companies all over the world, more than 218,000 -------, and its consolidated sales were about 14.9 trillion
4
yen in 2020.

Notes

· **ASIMO (Advanced Step in Innovative Mobility)** 人間の様な二足歩行が可能な世界初のロボット
· **HondaJet** 主翼の上にエンジンを搭載し燃費や乗り心地を向上させ小型ビジネスジェット機市場で販売世界一
  となった
· **consolidated sales** 連結売上高

1. (A) omissions

(B) relations

(C) emissions

(D) occupations

2. (A) cutting-edge

(B) customer-centered

(C) well-organized

(D) data-driven

3. (A) weapon

(B) robot

(C) text

(D) equipment

4. (A) subsidiaries

(B) factories

(C) employees

(D) employers

UNIT 3

Global Luxury Brand from Japan

Most Luxurious and Practical Accommodations

Imperial Hotel

In 1890, at the request of the Japanese government, the Imperial Hotel was founded to accommodate distinguished international visitors to Japan.

　帝国ホテルは1890年に、近代日本の迎賓館として海外の賓客をもてなす目的で開設された。今も日本を代表する最上級のホテルとしての役割を果たしている。これまで各国首脳の日本訪問時の宿泊先や、世界的な会議の会場としても活用されてきた。ホテルウエディング、バイキングレストラン、ランドリーサービスなど、帝国ホテルが始めたサービスが日本の高級ホテルの基準となっている。

Business Issue 日本のラグジュアリーホテルのブランドの発展に向けて

　定保は、2009 年に日本を代表する帝国ホテル東京の総支配人に就任した。ホテル業は災害などに影響を受けやすい。例えば 2011 年の東日本大震災の後、訪日外国人が激減した。帝国ホテルも宿泊客の 5 割が海外の顧客であるため影響を受けた。このような困難を乗り越え、定保は 2013 年に代表取締役社長に就任した。東京オリンピックや大阪万博など国際的なイベントを控え、様々な外資系の高級ホテルも日本に開業してきた。帝国ホテルは、これまでの伝統を守るだけでなく、グローバル化が一層進む中で、より強固なブランド力を構築する必要があった。

Warm-up

写真に関する英文を聞き学習の準備をしましょう。最も適切な選択肢を選びましょう。 2-01

(A)　　(B)　　(C)　　(D)

Vocabulary Input

次の英語に合う日本語を選び記号で答えましょう。 2-02

1. redesign （　　）
2. architect （　　）
3. resist earthquakes （　　）
4. evacuees （　　）
5. completion ceremony （　　）
6. Westernize Japan （　　）
7. solid construction （　　）

(A) 耐震となっている	(B) 日本を西洋化する	(C) 設計を見直す	(D) 建築家
(E) 避難者	(F) 強固な建設	(G) 竣工式	

80

Learning Important Expressions for Business Case Studies

ビジネスケースの理解に重要な表現に関連する下記の英文を完成させましょう。

1. The hotel was constructed to ------- important foreign visitors.

    (A) royal   (B) guest   (C) accommodate   (D) design

2. The Imperial Hotel had only minor damage ------- to its solid construction.

    (A) because   (B) as   (C) results   (D) thanks

3. The CEO took the ------- to visit domestic travel agencies.

    (A) indifference   (B) initiative   (C) incentive   (D) investigate

Listening Booster

企業情報に関する英文を聞いて背景を理解しましょう。 2-03

A. Listen and choose the best answer to each question.

1. How many guest rooms were there in the original building of the Imperial Hotel?

    (A) 54   (B) 60   (C) 260   (D) 772

2. Who was Frank Lloyd Wright?

    (A) The person who redesigned the Imperial Hotel in 1970

    (B) Someone who helped many people after the earthquake

    (C) A world-famous architect

    (D) A man who designed three hotels in Japan

3. How many people use the facilities each weekday?

    (A) 772   (B) 931   (C) 2,400   (D) 10,000

B. Listening Review

  Aの音声をもう一度聞き下の英文の（   ）に適切な表現を書き入れましょう。 2-04

The Most Prestigious Hotel in Japan

The original building of the Imperial Hotel had only 60 [1](   ) rooms and consisted of three floors. In 1923, the Imperial Hotel was rebuilt. The new hotel was designed by the world-famous [2](   ), Frank Lloyd Wright. Wright's design, which took four years to complete and cost six times the original estimate, included 260 guest rooms and a building that could resist earthquakes and fire. In 1970, the hotel was ³(   ) again. This design included 17 floors above ground, three floors below ground, and a new main building with 772 guest rooms. In 2019, there were 931 rooms, and more than 10,000 people used the ⁴(   ) each weekday. Moreover, the hotel group consisted of three hotels in Japan and had about 2,400 employees. The annual sales were 54.5 billion yen in 2019.

Notes

· **Frank Lloyd Wright** 米国を代表する世界的建築家

Learning From Authentic Business Examples

次の帝国ホテルに関する旅行ガイドのホームページを読んで以下の質問に答えましょう。 2-05〜07

For World Travelers
Where to Stay in Japan

The Imperial Hotel: Representing Japanese *Omotenashi*

During the Meiji period, the Japanese government tried to Westernize Japan. Accordingly, in 1890, the Imperial Hotel was constructed to accommodate important foreign visitors. Since then, the Imperial Hotel has not only been used as accommodation for important guests to Japan, but also as a stage for
5 international exchange and business meetings.

On the 1st of September, 1923, when preparations were being made for the completion ceremony for the second generation of the main building, the Great Kanto Earthquake struck Tokyo. While many buildings in the area were destroyed, the Imperial Hotel had only minor damage thanks to its solid
10 construction. As a result, the Imperial Hotel could accommodate evacuees, which it did, free of charge. It also provided temporary office space to embassies and news agencies. Additionally, because many shrines were also destroyed by the earthquake and there was no place to have weddings, the Imperial Hotel became the first hotel to offer hotel weddings in Japan. To do this, it set
15 up a shrine in the hotel so that the wedding ceremony and reception could both be held in the hotel.

There are other things that this hotel is famous for. For example, its laundry service, which started in 1910, had a very high reputation. Once a famous Hollywood star mentioned the service in a movie. Additionally, in 1957, it
20 opened the first buffet-style restaurant (known as "Viking" in Japan). Since then, this buffet style has become very popular, and many other restaurants have copied it.

CLICK HERE FOR MORE INFORMATION

· **the Great Kanto Earthquake** 関東大震災

本文の内容として正しい場合は T を、正しくない場合は F を（　）に書きましょう。

1. The Imperial Hotel has been used only as accommodation for important guests to Japan. (　　)

2. The hotel started hotel weddings because many shrines that were used for weddings were destroyed by the earthquake. (　　)

3. The hotel did not create Hollywood movies. (　　)

Reading Booster

帝国ホテルのビジネスケースを読んで内容を理解しましょう。　　　 2-08〜12

Global Leadership of a Luxury Hotel

Hideya Sadayasu joined the Imperial Hotel Group in 1984 and was assigned to the sales office in Los Angeles in 1991. He was in charge of a tremendously large territory, the western part of the U.S. Since it was before the Internet, Sadayasu had to pack his bags full of Imperial Hotel brochures and travel to all the local travel agencies by himself. His four years of hard work increased the number of guests from the United 5 States to the hotel by 20 percent.

Sadayasu was appointed International Manager of Sales in 2000 to increase the number of international guests to the hotel. Unfortunately, the terrorist attacks in the U.S. on September 11, 2001 occurred, and American guests, who make up 20 percent of the guests at the hotel, stopped coming. To cover this loss by attracting more domestic 10 customers to the hotel, he took the initiative to visit domestic travel agencies with his salespeople. Due to his and his team's efforts, they were able to overcome this crisis.

In 2009, Sadayasu became the general manager of the Imperial Hotel and

prepared to fight against global competition from overseas luxury hotel chains, such as
15 Ritz-Carlton. To compete with these hotels, the Imperial Hotel did a major renovation at a cost of 18 billion yen. Moreover, they reduced the number of guest rooms from 1,200 to 931 to enlarge individual room sizes and improve facilities.

When the Imperial Hotel held a 120th anniversary party on March 11, 2011, the Great East Japan Earthquake hit Tokyo. Sadayasu quickly set up an operations center
20 and spearheaded support for evacuees. The lobby and banquet halls were opened to accept 2,000 refugees. Additionally, the hotel provided blankets, bottled water, and food free of charge, while Sadayasu made and served vegetable soup for the refugees.

As a global strategy, Sadayasu opened the hotel's Singapore Office in 2014 to try and get customers from ASEAN markets. Due to the staff's effort in Singapore, the
25 number of visitors to the hotel in 2019 reached a record high of about 10,000 per day.

Notes

· **International Manager of Sales** 営業部国際課長
· **the terrorist attacks in the U.S. on September 11, 2001 occured,** 2001 年 9 月 11 日に起こった米国同時多発テロ事件
· **the general manager** 総支配人　· **Ritz-Carlton** 世界的な高級ホテルのリッツ・カールトン
· **the Great East Japan Earthquake** 東日本大震災
· **ASEAN (Association of Southeast Asian Nations)** 東南アジア諸国連合

1. Why did Mr. Sadayasu have to travel to local travel agencies by himself?

   (A) Because he needed to be in the U.S. for four years.

   (B) Because 20 percent of Imperial Hotel guests came from the U.S.

   (C) Because there was no Internet yet.

   (D) Because his territory was so large.

2. What caused a decrease in the number of international guests to the hotel?

   (A) a terrorist attack in America

   (B) new competition

   (C) Sadayasu's new appointment

   (D) problems with domestic travel agencies

3. Why did the Imperial Hotel reduce the number of its guest rooms to 931?

   (A) Because it did not have enough money for renovations.

   (B) Because it had to open a new hotel in Singapore.

   (C) Because the Great East Japan Earthquake hit Tokyo.

   (D) Because it wanted to make its rooms bigger.

A **Business Focus:** ビジネス英語を学ぼう！

Definition of Luxury Brand

There are five significant elements to a luxury brand. They are as follows:

1. Craftsmanship and high quality: 職人芸のような優れた品質
2. Rarity and high price: 稀少で高価
3. Strong brand identity: 強いブランド・アイデンティティ
4. Tradition, history, and anecdotes: 伝統や歴史と逸話
5. Celebrity service: セレブのようなサービスを顧客に提供する

Tradition and Innovation

Luxury brands should not only maintain tradition but should also enhance high-value innovation.

ラグジュアリー・ブランドであるためには、伝統を守りながら、一方で高付加価値の
ある革新も行わなければならない。

B ビジネス英語の理解を深めよう！

Luxury business に関する以下の例文を与えられた文字に続くように空所をうめて完成させましょ
う。この際、本文を再度確認し、関連する他の事象にも下線を引き **C** のタスクにも活用できるよう
にしましょう。

1. Its (*l*　　　　　　) service, which started in 1910, has a very high (*r*　　　　　　).

2. The hotel (*r*　　　　　) the number of guest rooms from 1,200 to 931 to
(*e*　　　　　) individual room sizes and improve (*f*　　　　　).

3. The hotel has been used as a (*s*　　　　　) for international (*e*　　　　　) and
business (*m*　　　　　).

4. In 1890, the Imperial Hotel was constructed to (*a*　　　　　) important foreign
(*v*　　　　　).

5. The Imperial Hotel did a major (*r*　　　　　) at a cost of 18 (*b*　　　　　) yen.

C Business Discussion

B の表現を参考にして、次のテーマについてクラスメートと話し合いましょう。

What are the examples of the five luxury elements of the Imperial Hotel?

• Craftsmanship and high quality

_____

_____

_____

• Rarity and high price

_____

_____

_____

• Strong brand identity

_____

_____

_____

• Tradition, history, and anecdotes

_____

_____

_____

• Celebrity service

_____

_____

_____

Creating a Japanese Luxury Brand

Chapter 10

Toyota Lexus

It was essential to develop a cool image for Lexus.

　トヨタ自動車は創業初期の段階で、自動車の大量生産方式を最初に開発し成功した米国フォード社から車体の生産技術を学んだ。また、自動車販売のマーケティングを確立し世界一の販売を記録したゼネラル・モータース社からマーケティング戦略を学んだ。やがてトヨタは大衆車の製造販売で世界の評価を得たが、高級車市場では苦戦を強いられていた。

1989 年に米国市場に高級車として投入されたレクサスは、トヨタの最高技術を結集した高品質の製品であり富裕層の支持を得た。1999 年から 2010 年まで連続して北米の高級車販売で 1 位を記録した。日本でも 2005 年に発売が開始され、高級感のある専門のディーラーや、最高の接客が支持を得て売り上げも伸びた。だが、グローバルではベンツや BMW に比べると高級車としてのブランド力に問題を抱えていた。また、次第に購入者の年齢層も高くなり、将来の購入者である若者にもブランドを訴求しなければならない。これらの問題を解決すべく、高田はレクサスのブランドマネージメント部の部長に就任した。

Warm-up

写真に関する英文を聞き学習の準備をしましょう。最も適切な選択肢を選びましょう。 🎧 2-13

(A)　　(B)　　(C)　　(D)

Vocabulary Input

次の英語に合う日本語を選び記号で答えましょう。 🎧 2-14

1. cheap and poorly made　　(　)
2. suspend　　(　)
3. manufacturing procedures　　(　)
4. passenger cars　　(　)
5. wealthy people　　(　)
6. dealers　　(　)
7. customer service　　(　)
8. restructure　　(　)

| (A) 富裕層 | (B) 製造手順 | (C) 自動車販売店 | (D) 安かろう悪かろう |
| (E) 顧客サービス | (F) 乗用車 | (G) 延期する | (H) 再構築する |

ビジネスケースの理解に重要な表現に関連する下記の英文を完成させましょう。

1. Once Japanese cars were regarded as being cheap and ------- made.

    (A) richly   (B) quick   (C) poorly   (D) substantially

2. ------- having an excellent reputation for small cars, Toyota could not appeal to wealthy people.

    (A) Though   (B) Although   (C) However   (D) Despite

3. The new sports car became the company's ------- model.

    (A) flagship   (B) fashion   (C) greedy   (D) attraction

Listening Booster

企業情報に関する英文を聞いて背景を理解しましょう。 2-15

A. Listen and choose the best answer to each question.

  1. What did people think of Toyota cars in 1937?

    (A) They were expensive.

    (B) They were made by GM.

    (C) They were unreliable.

    (D) They were manufactured in the U.S.

  2. How did Toyota become the top imported car in the U.S. in 1975?

    (A) It created a joint venture.

    (B) It created quality cars that were popular.

    (C) It stopped manufacturing cars in Japan.

    (D) It stopped selling passenger cars in the U.S.

B. Listening Review

  A の音声をもう一度聞き下の英文の（　　　　）に適切な表現を書き入れましょう。 2-16

Becoming a World-leading Company With Continuous Improvement

A: Toyota Motor Corporation was founded in 1937. Was it reliable from the beginning?

B: Unfortunately, its cars were [1](   ) as being cheap and poorly made.

A: Really?

B: Yes. For example, in 1961, the company's quality problems, which resulted in weak sales, made Toyota suspend exports of [2](   ) cars.

A: However, Toyota improved its manufacturing procedures and introduced effective techniques such as the Just in Time System, or JIT, and Total Quality Control, or TQC, right?

B: Yes. These efforts led to Toyota becoming the top imported car in the U.S. in 1975. Then, in 1984, it set up a joint [3](   ) with GM and started producing cars in the U.S.

A: It's become a global company since then.

B: Indeed. By 2019, the Toyota group had sold more than 10.7 million cars, and it was the world [4](   ) in global car sales in the first half of 2020.

A: That's why its annual revenue is as huge as 275.4 billion US dollars.

Notes

· **Just in Time System** トヨタ自動車が確立した製造過程の効率化を最大限にするシステム
· **Total Quality Control** 製造だけでなく、営業・企画・総務など非製造部門も含め、全社的に製品の質を高める運動

▶ Learning From Authentic Business Examples ▮▮▮

Lexus のビジネスレポートに関する英文に関する質問に答えましょう。　 2-17〜19

WORLD BUSINESS REPORT

Luxury Car From the U.S.

Toyota could not appeal to wealthy people who were fans of German cars, like Mercedes Benz. To attract wealthy customers, Toyota collected its most capable engineers and set up the Tahara plant to develop luxury cars. This plant was the most computerized and robotized in the
5 world. These efforts led to the production of Lexus, which has similar quality and safety to German luxury cars. Furthermore, to increase the appeal of Lexus, it was priced at $35,000. The German competitors' cars typically sold for $40,000 to $60,000.

In order to operate in the luxury car business, Toyota initially selected
10 only 81 dealers out of a possible 1,600. These dealerships were located in attractive buildings and had sales staff who were trained in how to provide excellent customer service. These efforts to create a luxury brand worked. Lexus appealed to baby boomers. In the first year of sales in 1989, Toyota sold 16,300 cars, which was the highest number of sales for a new
15 car in the U.S. In fact, many celebrities became Lexus owners, such as Bill

Gates, the founder of Microsoft, and Steven Spielberg, the famous film director.

After the great success of Lexus in the U.S., Toyota launched the model in Japan in 2005. Although, initially, Lexus sold well in Japan, sales were less than expected. This was because the Toyota brand 20 was so familiar to the Japanese. Thus, to bring attention to the Lexus, Toyota simply raised the price of the car.

Notes

· **Mercedes Benz** 富裕層が好んで購入するドイツの自動車メーカー
· **Tahara plant** レクサスの製造のために設立された愛知県にある工場
· **computerized and robotized** コンピュータやロボットで制御された製造過程
· **baby boomers** 第二次世界大戦後から 1964 年頃までの出生率の高い世代で購買力があるとされる

本文の内容として正しい場合は T を、正しくない場合は F を（　）に書きましょう。

1. The price of Lexus was at least $5,000 cheaper than cars made by German competitors.

（　　）

2. Toyota initially selected 1,600 dealers to develop attractive buildings.　　（　　）

3. Lexus sold well in Japan because the Toyota brand was so familiar to the Japanese.

（　　）

Reading Booster

次の Lexus のビジネスケースを読んで内容を理解しましょう。　　2-20〜24

Lexus Should be Cooler Than Audi Within 3 Years

In Europe, Japanese cars were known for being economical and reliable. As a result, it was difficult for Toyota to be competitive in the luxury car market there. Moreover, because American Lexus owners were baby boomers, the car was seen as an older person's car. Thus, the car did not attract younger people.

To overcome this stagnation, Toyota restructured to create a new and 5 independent organization, Lexus International. This was done in 2012. During this restructuring, Atsushi Takada was appointed as Director of Lexus Brand Management, a division that works to control and develop Lexus so that it becomes a consistent global brand from Japan.

Takada's team carefully examined Lexus's weakness by comparing it with 10 competitors. They found that it was essential to develop a cool image for the car. As a result, their goal was that "Lexus should be cooler than Audi within three years."

Accordingly, Lexus was redesigned with a spindle-shaped grille. This new design resulted in a new Lexus model, the LC sports car. The LC sports car became the company's
15 flagship model.

In addition to this major model change, Takada carried out a series of innovative promotional activities. He produced many cutting-edge commercials and made the best use of INTERSECT BY LEXUS as a space for experiencing and publicizing the Lexus brand. He also created the Lexus Fashion Award in Salone del Mobile.Milano in Italy,
20 which supports talented young designers.

These luxury marketing campaigns contributed to the development of a cool image for Lexus. In fact, the word "cool" related to Lexus was used 4.3 times more in 2014 than 2012. Furthermore, the percentage of customers who recognized Lexus as a cool brand increased from 43 percent to 48 percent in Japan and 51 percent to 61 percent
25 in the U.S. during the period from 2013 to 2015. At the same time, the average age of Lexus customers decreased by three years in Japan. During this same period, global sales of Lexus increased from 500,000 to 650,000. In 2019, the number reached 765, 271.

| **Notes** |

· **stagnation** 停滞した状況
· **Lexus International** トヨタ社長が直轄する、他の部門とは独立したグローバルでレクサスの開発やマーケティング、販売を統括する組織
· **spindle-shaped grille** 紡績機の糸を巻き取る軸の形状を車のフロントマスクのデザインとしている
· **INTERSECT BY LEXUS** 東京の青山、ニューヨーク、アラブ首長国連邦のデュバイに設置され、既存のショールームとは異なり、高級レストランやデザイナー商品販売、イベント会場の機能を持つ施設
· **Salone del Mobile.Milano** 1961 年から毎年ミラノで開催される世界最大規模を持つ家具の見本市

1. Why did Toyota have difficulty entering the luxury car market in Europe?

(A) Because its cars were popular with young people.

(B) Because its cars were unreliable.

(C) Because there was a car boom in Europe at the time.

(D) Because its cars were thought of as economical.

2. What did Toyota NOT do to improve its brand image in 2012?

(A) It restructured.

(B) It created Lexus International.

(C) It copied Audi.

(D) It appointed Takada.

3. What happened as a result of the luxury marketing campaigns for Lexus?

   (A) Lexus car sales went from 650,000 to 500,000.

   (B) Lexus was more popular than two years before.

   (C) Lexus's popularity increased from 51 percent to 61 percent in Japan.

   (D) The average age of Lexus customers in Japan rose by three years.

▶ Tasks for Business Studies

A Business Focus: ビジネス英語を学ぼう！

Just in Time System (JIT) and Total Quality Control (TQC)

Many Japanese companies have introduced the Just in Time System and Total Quality Control and established the most reliable brand image in the world.

製造過程で徹底的に無駄を省き、効率化を追求するカンバン方式とも呼ばれる JIT や、全ての部門の社員が協力して改善に取り組む TQC などを多くの企業が取り入れ、日本ブランドは品質の高いものとして世界的に認知された。

Lexus should be cooler than Audi within three years

The Lexus brand manager enhanced the effective marketing strategies named "Lexus should be cooler than Audi within three years."

トヨタ車を購入していた顧客は、経済的に余裕ができると高級なイメージを持つドイツ車等に乗り換える傾向があった。このためレクサスは、具体的な目標として 3 年以内にドイツのアウディ車を超える、クールなブランドになるという目標を立て戦略を実行した。

レクサス高級ブランド形成に関する以下の例文を与えられた文字に続くように空所をうめて完成させましょう。この際、本文を再度確認し、関連する他の事象にも下線を引き C のタスクにも活用できるようにしましょう。

1. Toyota collected its most capable (e   ) and set up the Tahara (p   )
   to develop luxury cars to attract (u   ) customers.

2. Many (c   ) became Lexus (o   ), such as Bill Gates, the founder
   of Microsoft, and Steven Spielberg, the (f   ) film director.

3. He (c   ) produced cutting-edge CMs and made the best (u   ) of
   INTERSECT BY LEXUS as a space for experiencing and (p   ) the Lexus
   brand.

4. The percentage of customers who (r   ) Lexus as a (c   ) brand
   (i   ) from 43 percent to 48 percent in Japan.

C Business Discussion

B の表現を参考にして、次のテーマについてクラスメートと話し合いましょう。

How does Lexus develop luxury marketing?

• Craftsmanship

_____

_____

• Celebrity

_____

_____

• Promotion

_____

_____

• New Branding

_____

_____

The Species That Survives is the One That is the Most Adaptable to Change

Tashiro Alloy Inc.

鮨 和魂／フォーシーズンズホテル京都　設計：STRICKLAND

株式会社 田代合金所
TASHIRO ALLOY INC.

SEMs (small and medium-sized enterprises) can survive recessions because they are able to respond quickly to unpredictable economic fluctuations. Moreover, they can explore new business opportunities more easily than large companies.

　田代合金所は新聞社などの活字用合金の製造をしていた。しかし、時代の変化と共に技術力を活かしたイノベーション行い、新たな分野を開拓してきた。特に近年は、大企業が取り組めない手作りの芸術品を創造し、ラグジュアリー分野のビジネスを行っている。

Business Issue　変化を続けて生き残る

　1914 年開業の田代合金所は当初、新聞社などの活字用合金の製造をしていた。だがやがて印刷技術が発展し、活字用合金の需要はなくなると思われた。そのため、金属を溶かして精密な製品を作る技術を活かし、自動車の特殊な部品や半導体用メタルを開発していった。しかし、新たに社長に就任した田邊は、大企業に製品を納入する下請け業務だけでは限界があると考えていた。ある日、錫を板状に加工する際に、いつものように均一でなく、わざと歪めると、表面に面白い模様が浮かび上がってきた。これを何かの製品に使う方法はないかと考えた。

Warm-up

写真に関する英文を聞き学習の準備をしましょう。最も適切な選択肢を選びましょう。　 2-25

(A)　　(B)　　(C)　　(D)

Vocabulary Input

次の英語に合う日本語を選び記号で答えましょう。　 2-26

1. economic disparities 　　(　　)
2. subcontractor 　　(　　)
3. go bankrupt 　　(　　)
4. economic fluctuation 　　(　　)
5. unpredictable 　　(　　)
6. alloys 　　(　　)
7. sales agent 　　(　　)

(A) 経済変動	(B) 予測不可能な	(C) 経済格差	(D) 下請け業者
(E) 取引代理店	(F) 倒産する	(G) 合金	

ビジネスケースの理解に重要な表現に関連する下記の英文を完成させましょう。

1. Companies will not go ------- if they do not have debts.

   (A) abroad   (B) backward   (C) bankrupt   (D) mad

2. The CEO discovered a new business opportunity when ------- tin plates.

   (A) product   (B) production   (C) produced   (D) producing

3. The manager ------- the business overseas.

   (A) decided to expand   (B) decided expanding   (C) deciding expansion

   (D) decided expansion

Listening Booster

ビジネスに関するチャットの会話を聞いて質問に答えましょう。   CD 2-27

A. Listen and choose the best answer to each question.

1. What does the woman mention about Japan?

   (A) That there are many large companies

   (B) That there are too many SMEs

   (C) That small companies outnumber medium-sized companies

   (D) That there are relatively small number of large companies

2. What is a benefit of SMEs for large companies?

   (A) Using SMEs helps protect them in a recession.

   (B) Large companies can protect SMEs during a recession.

   (C) SMEs can use large companies as subcontractors.

   (D) Large companies can subcontract with other large companies.

B. Listening Review

　Aの音声をもう一度聞き下の英文の（　　　　）に適切な表現を書き入れましょう。   CD 2-28

Jonathan [2:40 PM]

Shall we discuss issues related to small and medium-sized enterprises in Japan?

Janette [2:42 PM]

Sure. In Japan there are not so many large companies, but there are many small and medium-sized [1]( ) called SMEs.

Jonathan [2:45 PM]

There are various economic disparities between these two groups. Is this correct?

Janette [2:48 PM]

That's right. SMEs often [2]( ) parts manufacturing and product processing as subcontractors of large companies.

Jonathan [2:52 PM]

It is said that large corporations value SMEs because large corporations can save capital and take [3]( ) of the lower wages at SMEs.

Janette [2:26 PM]

Unfortunately, it is correct. Additionally, during recessions, SMEs can be used to protect large companies from the economic fluctuations that occur, such as [4]( ) in orders and unit price drops.

> ## Learning From Authentic Business Examples

田代合金所のビジネスケースに関する英文を読んで後の問いに答えなさい。   2-29~32

BUSINESS REPORT ONLINE | **ECONOMY**

Small but Sustainable Company with Innovation

When alloy type was replaced by optical type in the 1960s, Tashiro Alloy needed to change their manufacturing focus. In 1965, the company used their advanced casting technology to produce alloys called cast metal for accessories, jewelry, and toy figurines.

5 　　In 1985, Mr. Toyohiro Tanabe developed a music accessory made from lead ingots to reduce the vibration of speakers. He called these ingots TG Metal and began selling them to consumers. Tashiro Alloy had never sold alloy products to consumers before that. However, Tanabe was convinced that consumers like himself who loved music

10 would appreciate TG Metal. He traveled all over Japan to negotiate with audio product specialty stores that were advertising in audio magazines. He got them to become sales agents. In fact, TG Metal is still popular today and is sold on Amazon.

　　During the Japanese asset price bubble from 1986 to 1991,

15 many CEOs of SMEs used their companies' profits to invest in real

---

98

estate and the stock market. However, Tanabe recognized one important rule of business. That is, companies will not go bankrupt if they do not have debts. Therefore, he used the company's surplus funds to repay their entire bank loan. This was wise because when the asset price bubble broke in 1992, the company did not suffer 20 bankruptcy as other SMEs did.

Unfortunately, from the mid-1990s, the domestic cast metal market shrank, and manufacturing bases began moving to China. Accordingly, the company had to explore new business opportunities to survive, which they did. Tashiro Alloy started producing many new 25 products, including semiconductor metals and fishing accessories.

SHARE THIS ARTICLE:

Notes

· **type** 活字　　· **optical type** 光学印刷　　· **cast metal** 鋳造金属　　· **lead ingots** 鉛延べ金のかたまり
· **vibration** 防振　　· **asset price bubble** バブル経済

本文の内容として正しい場合は T を、正しくない場合は F を（　）に書きましょう。

1. Tashiro Alloy developed a music accessory in 1965.　　　　　　　　　（　　）

2. TG Metal is a music accessory which is still popular and sold on the Internet.　（　　）

3. Tashiro Alloy moved to China to produce many new products, including semiconductor metals.　　　　　　　　　　　　　　　　　　　　　（　　）

Reading Booster

田代合金所のビジネスケースを読んで質問に答えましょう。　　　 2-33～36

Developing an Arts and Crafts Business

Coincidentally, Tanabe discovered a new business opportunity when producing tin plates differently from traditional methods. Usually, producing tin plates requires very clean and flat working surfaces so that plates can be made without any defects. In fact, many companies spend large amounts of time and energy to develop the technology to produce perfect plates. However, once Tanabe purposely made a distorted pattern on 5 a tin plate. To his surprise, the pattern looked like a work of art. The distorted surface revealed many different patterns when light reflected on it from different angles. This gave him the idea to make interior tiles, so he consulted with an interior designer.

In 2003, he established a new technology to produce cast metal sheets of molded
10 tin tiles with artistic designs. The product, named Cornwall, is handmade, and requires
precision technology to melt and flow various metals in a furnace. Moreover, this process
is impossible and unprofitable for large companies to copy in their large-scale production
lines.

In Japan, Cornwall became popular and was used in first class restaurants in
15 luxury hotels in Tokyo and Kyoto. Due to this success, Tanabe decided to expand the
business overseas, and he succeeded. The tiles were used in several projects and were
exhibited in trade fairs. Moreover, Tashiro Alloy won the Blueprint Award at 100%Design
London in 2009. Now, the company operates businesses in the EU, U.S., and UAE.

Being located in Asakusa, Tokyo means that Tashiro Alloy is near to one of
20 Japan's most prestigious art schools, Tokyo University of Arts. This gave Tanabe the
opportunity to meet a distinguished forging artist, Tomoya Tachibana. Together, they
collaborated on a project to create luxurious interior decorating materials called
Tachibana in 2014. Tachibana are very artistic and highly valued and can be seen at the
headquarters of a jewelry company in Tokyo.

Notes

· **distorted** 歪んだ　·**distorted pattern** 歪んだ模様　·**furnace** 溶解炉
· **Blueprint Award at 100%Design London** 100%Design London は毎年開催される建築・デザインを扱う英
国最大の展示会。Blueprint Award はその年の優れた建築やデザインを表彰する賞
· **forging artist** 金属板に文様を打ち込む芸術家
· **Tachibana** 田代合金所の製造したコンウォールに、芸儒家である橘智哉氏が特殊技術である綾打ちを施した高
級製品

1. What is NOT needed to produce tin plates?

(A) a flat surface 　　　　　(B) lots of time

(C) a clean working area 　　(D) many technicians

2. Why is Cornwall difficult for large companies to copy?

(A) Because it is handmade, which is unprofitable for large
companies.

(B) Because it is produced in furnaces that are too expensive.

(C) Because large-scale productions lines are too precise.

(D) Because large companies cannot melt metals.

3. What is unique about Tachibana?

(A) They are mass-produced.

(B) They are made at a prestigious art school.

(C) They are the result of a collaboration.

(D) They are made of pearls.

田代合金所ショールーム
撮影：丸子成明

A Business Focus: ビジネス英語を学ぼう！

Small and medium-sized enterprises (SMEs)
SMEs play a significant role in the Japanese economy. They represent more than 99 percent of all enterprises and about 70 percent of all employment.
日本の企業のうち 99% は中小企業で、全労働者の 70%がそこで働いている。日本の産業において重要な役割を占めている。

Luxury Business: Craftsmanship, Rarity, High Price, and Episode
今回のケースのラグジュアリー・ビジネスに必要な要素は手作りの匠の技、希少性、高価、エピソードである。

B Business Discussion：ビジネス英語の理解を深めよう！

What kinds of products has Tashiro Alloy made?
1965 年の例を参考にして下の表に製品名と説明を書き入れましょう。

History of Tashiro Alloy

Year	Product
1965	*The company used their advanced casting technology to produce alloys called cast metal for accessories, jewelry, and toy figurines.*
1985	*TG Metal*
2003	Cornwall
2014	

C Business Discussion

Bの表現を参考にして、次のテーマについてクラスメートと話し合いましょう。

How did Tashiro Alloy Inc. develop its luxury business?

_____

_____

_____

_____

_____

_____

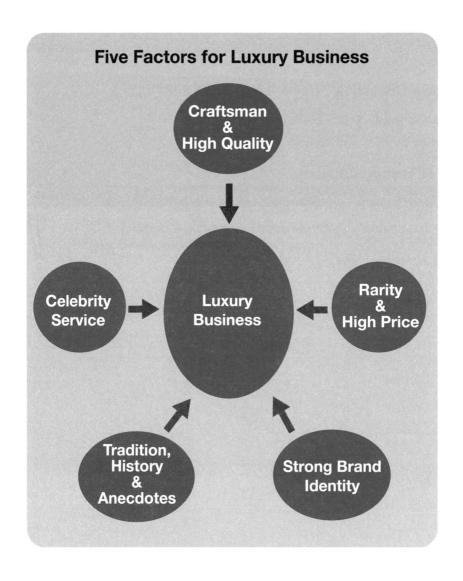

Review Unit 3

Chapter9−11 の復習をしましょう

1 最も適切な応答の選択肢を選びましょう。 2-37～39

Listen to the question or statement and three responses. Then choose the best answer.

   1. (A) (B) (C)

   2. (A) (B) (C)

   3. (A) (B) (C)

2 レクスサスの世界の販売台数に関するグラフの説明を聞いて質問に
答えましょう。 CD 2-40

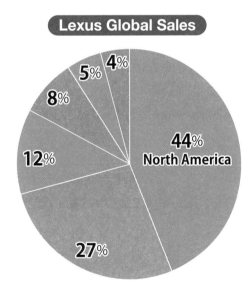

Lexus Global Sales

- 44% North America
- 27%
- 12%
- 8%
- 5%
- 4%

Note : Lexus divides the global market into 6 areas: North America, Japan, China, East Asia, Middle East, and Europe.

1. Which number represents the percentage of total sales in the Chinese market?

(A) 44%   (B) 27%

(C) 12%   (D) 8%

2. How many Lexus cars are sold in Europe?

(A) 44,000   (B) 12,000

(C) 87,000   (D) 62,000

3. Which area is NOT mentioned in the announcement?

(A) China   (B) Europe

(C) Japan   (D) East Asia

3 下の博物館の地図に関する説明文を聞いて質問に対する最も適切な選 🎧 2-41
択肢を選びましょう。

1. Who most likely is the speaker?

(A) a receptionist   (B) a salesperson

(C) a tour guide   (D) a museum constructor

2. Where can you see toy figurines?

(A) Room 1   (B) Room 2   (C) Room 3   (D) Cafeteria

3. Where is the shop located on the map below?

(A) A   (B) B   (C) C   (D) D

UNIT 4

Global Business with Sustainable Development Goals

BOP Business Enhancing Sustainable Development Goals

Chapter 12

Yamaha Motor's business in Indonesia and Africa

Yamaha Motor's corporate mission is to promote sustainable societies where it operates business overseas.

　ヤマハ発動機は、世界に 111 の関連会社を持ち、180 以上の国と地域でビジネスを行っている。2019 年には海外の売上が全体の約 90％に達している。売上の内訳はオートバイが 60％で船外機が 20％を占めている。アジアやアフリカの新興国や途上国でも現地に根差した営業活動を行っている。これらの地域は、安全な水が十分に確保できない国も多かった。この問題を解決するために、ヤマハ・クリーンウォーターを開発した。

Business Issue　途上国に命の水を

　2020年の時点で世界では20億もの人が安全な水を手に入れることができない。これらの多くは途上国や新興国の農村部で、汚染水による疫病に苦しんだり、子供が水汲みの重労働に従事しており、大きな社会問題となっている。だが貧しい国々は水道を整備する技術も資金も乏しい。ヤマハ発動機はオートバイ生産工場をインドネシアに設立したが、現地の水の衛生問題に直面した。抜本的な解決のために、水を浄化する装置を自ら開発することになった。

Warm-up

写真に関する英文を聞き学習の準備をしましょう。最も適切な選択肢を選びましょう。　CD 2-42

(A)　　(B)　　(C)　　(D)

Vocabulary Input

次の英語に合う日本語を選び記号で答えましょう。　CD 2-43

1. corporate mission　　　　（　　　）

2. total annual revenue　　（　　　）

3. developing countries　　（　　　）

4. guarantee　　　　　　　（　　　）

5. specialized technicians　（　　　）

6. water purification　　　（　　　）

7. unsanitary conditions　　（　　　）

(A) 保証する　　(B) 水の浄化　　(C) 企業理念　　(D) 途上国
(E) 不衛生な状況　(F) 特別な技術者　(G) 年の総収入

ビジネスケースの理解に重要な表現に関連する下記の英文を完成させましょう。

1. Yamaha Motor's corporate mission is to promote ------- societies.

   (A) suspectable   (B) support   (C) subscription   (D) sustainable

2. Yamaha Motor started a new research and ------- project.

   (A) develop   (B) development   (C) developed   (D) developing

3. Yamaha Motor did not begin ------- overseas until 1958.

   (A) expanding   (B) being expanded

   (C) having expanded   (D) to be expanded

Listening Booster

企業情報に関する英文を聞いて背景を理解しましょう。 2-44

A. Listen and choose the best answer to each question.

1. How well did Yamaha Motor do in developing countries?

   (A) It had much difficulty.   (B) It was an early leader.

   (C) It was a latecomer.   (D) It was not successful.

2. How much of Yamaha Motor's revenue comes from overseas operations?

   (A) 1.6 trillion yen   (B) more than 180 countries and regions

   (C) about 1.4 trillion yen   (D) 90 percent, and more than 1.6 trillion yen

B. Listening Review

Aの音声をもう一度聞き下の英文の（　　　　）に適切な表現を書き入れましょう。 2-45

A: Yamaha Motor did not begin expanding their business [1](   ) until 1958.

B: Yes, that's correct but, in a short time, it developed a reputation for being a pioneer in starting business in [2](   ) countries.

A: Sounds interesting. How is its current global business?

B: By 2019, it had created 111 overseas [3](   ) and was doing business in more than 180 countries and regions.

A: That's amazing. It does business in so many countries.

B: Furthermore, its total annual [4](   ) was 1.6 trillion yen, with 90 percent of that coming from overseas operations.

YAMAHA MOTOR のビジネスケースに関するジャーナルを読んで内容を理解しましょう。   2-46〜48

Journal of Business in Emerging countries

Developing a User- and Nature-friendly Clean Water System

　　Yamaha Motor has developed a home-use water purification system to improve living conditions for Japanese employees and their families who are sent to developing countries, such as Indonesia. This system, the OH 300, was developed in 1991. The OH 300 was the result of five years of research and development and
5 uses sand and carbon filters to purify water. Moreover, Yamaha Motor has established an advanced water testing laboratory, which guarantees very pure and safe water.

　　A member of Yamaha Motor's motorcycle manufacturing factory in Indonesia tried to sell the OH 300 in other countries. Unfortunately, the OH 300 cost $2,000 to buy and needed $200 for annual maintenance, which was too expensive for
10 ordinary people. Accordingly, the system could only be marketed to the rich or Japanese families who valued clean drinking water.

　　As a result of the development of the OH 300, Yamaha Motor's Japanese staff and their families did not need to worry about poor drinking water anymore. However, almost half of the local employees who worked for Yamaha Motor in
15 developing countries often live in undeveloped villages which have no public water services. They live in unsanitary conditions and only have access to river water. As Yamaha Motor's corporate mission is to promote sustainable societies where they operate business, they wanted to solve the water problems for people living in
20 undeveloped villages. At first, Yamaha Motor tried to use the OH 300, but it did not work well. This is because the system is for tap water, not dirty river water.

Notes

· **home-use water purification systems** 家庭用浄水器
· **OH 300** ヤマハ発動機が開発した新興国向けの家庭用浄水器
· **sand and carbon filters** 砂と活性炭フィルター

本文の内容として正しい場合はTを、正しくない場合はFを（　）に書きましょう。

1. Yamaha Motor started to develop a water purification system in Indonesia because the Indonesian government asked for support. 　　　　　　　　　　　（　　）

2. The OH 300 cost $2,000 to buy and needed $200 for annual maintenance, which was reasonable for Japanese families who valued clean drinking water. 　　　　（　　）

3. The OH 300 did not work well in undeveloped villages because it is for tap water, not dirty river water. 　　　　　　　　　　　　　　　　　　　　　　　　（　　）

Reading Booster

次のYAMAHA MOTORのビジネスケースを読んで内容を理解しましょう。 2-49〜51

BOP (Base of the Economic Pyramid) Business

In the mid-1990s, Yamaha Motor started a new research and development project to make a water-purification system for undeveloped villages. It wanted to develop a system that could clean the surface water from rivers and lakes. In 2000s, Yamaha Motor developed the Yamaha Clean Water Supply System (YCWSS) in Indonesia. As a result of this pilot plant, Yamaha Motor was able to develop a water 5 purification system that uses a slow sand filtration method to purify water. This method is similar to how water is purified in nature. The system has a simple design and is very compact. Also, it does not require annual filter replacement or maintenance by specialized technicians. In addition, the system does not need much electricity to operate, and it is possible to power the system with solar panels. 10

Although this system is ideal for developing countries, many rural communities do not have the budgets to install it by themselves. Thus, Yamaha Motor developed a unique business model. It formed partnerships with a variety of different funding organizations, like the United Nations Development Programme (UNDP). Additionally, Yamaha Motor recruited other organizations in Japan to help fund clean-water systems 15 for underdeveloped villages. For example, it recruited support from the Japanese Ministry of Foreign Affairs, the Japanese Ministry of Economy, Trade, and Industry (METI), JICA, and JETRO.

Yamaha Motor's goal is to let local communities become independent water business operators. Yamaha Motor helps communities set up individual local water 20 committees which operate the system and sell the water at a reasonable price. The money collected is then used for sustainable development. Yamaha Motor members frequently visit communities and voluntarily support the committees whenever they need help with problems. In 2020, in total, 41 YCWSS were successfully operating to improve peoples' lives with clean water in 14 different countries in Asia and Africa.

Notes

· **Yamaha Clean Water Supply System (YCWSS)** ヤマハ発動機の河川の水を浄水する途上国向けプラント
· **United Nations Development Programme (UNDP)** 国連開発計画
· **JICA (the Japan International Cooperation Agency)** 独立行政法人国際協力機構
· **JETRO (Japan External Trade Organization)** 日本貿易振興機構

1. How does the Yamaha Clean Water Supply System purify water?

(A) It uses water deep below the surface of rivers and lakes.

(B) It uses disposable filters.

(C) It uses sand to purify the water.

(D) It requires a pilot to clean the water.

2. What prevents rural communities from using the Yamaha Clean Water Supply System?

(A) the high cost

(B) the poor quality of the system

(C) the complexity of the system

(D) damage to nature

3. Which organization does NOT support Yamaha Motor's unique business model?

(A) Japanese Ministry of Foreign Affairs

(B) Japan International Trade Organization

(C) Japanese Ministry of Economy, Trade, and Industry

(D) United Nations Development Programme

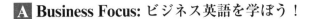

Tasks for Business Studies

A Business Focus: ビジネス英語を学ぼう！

SDGs : Sustainable of Development Goals

Private companies need to play a proactive role in the global effort to achieve SDGs.

2030 年までに貧困の撲滅、地球の保護、全人類の平和と豊かさの享受など 17 のゴールを達成するという国連で採択された目標。企業は単に自社の利益を求めるのでなく、SDGs に沿った社会への貢献が求められている。

BOP Business: Base of the Economic Pyramid Business

Private companies should design products and services for sustainable development that are useful and affordable for people who live in harsh conditions in developing countries.

世界人口の 72%を占める約 40 億人は、年間所得が 3,000 米ドル未満の貧困層で、主に開発途上国に住む。これらの地域を対象に NGO や多国籍企業が協力して持続可能なビジネスモデルを発展させることを目指している。

B ビジネス英語の理解を深めよう！

BOP Business に関する以下の例文を与えられた文字に続くように空所をうめて完成させましょう。この際、本文を再度確認し、関連する他の事象にも下線を引き C のタスクにも活用できるようにしましょう。

1. Yamaha Motor wanted to (s   ) the (w   ) problems for people living in undeveloped (v   ).

2. It wanted to develop a (s   ) that could clean the (s   ) water from rivers and (l   ).

3. The system has a simple (d   ) and is very (c   ), which is ideal for (d   ) countries.

4. The systems are successfully operating to (i   ) peoples' lives with (c   ) water in 14 different countries in Asia and (A   ).

C Business Discussion

B の表現を参考にして、次のテーマについてクラスメートと話し合いましょう。

How does Yamaha Motor organize the BOP business?

1. Where?

_____

_____

2. Why?

_____

_____

3. What?

_____

_____

4. Outcomes

_____

_____

Connecting People with What's Happening

Chapter 13

Twitter's goal is to create an social media that allows users to send short, quick messages anytime and anywhere.

　2006 年にジャック・ドーシーにより、ネット上で 140 文字の範囲でメッセージを交換する Twitter が始められた。だれでも、いつでも簡単に情報を伝えられるこのサービスは、瞬く間に世界に広がり、2020 年には世界で毎日 2 億人以上が利用している。だが、簡単に情報が送られるため、フェイクニュースや、中傷に使われるなど、予想できなかった課題を抱えるようになった。現代の重要な社会的コミュニケーションのインフラとして発展しつつ、様々な問題を解決していく必要があった。

Twitter は素早くコミュニケーションができるツールとして広く活用され、若者を中心に社会的なインフラとなっている。だが、世界中で利用者が増えると、中には不適切な使い方もされ始めた。さらにフェイクニュースの発信や、政治家による扇動にも使われた。2014 年に日本法人の代表になった笹本は、これらの課題を解決し、利用者に信頼されるメディアを構築しなければならなかった。

▶ **Warm-up**

写真に関する英文を聞き学習の準備をしましょう。最も適切な選択肢を選びましょう。　🎧 2-52

(A)　　(B)　　(C)　　(D)

▶ **Vocabulary Input**

次の英語に合う日本語を選び記号で答えましょう。　🎧 2-53

1. active users　　　　　　　　　　　　（　　）
2. public interest　　　　　　　　　　　（　　）
3. fake news　　　　　　　　　　　　　（　　）
4. social communication infrastructure　（　　）
5. social responsibilities　　　　　　　（　　）
6. major media　　　　　　　　　　　　（　　）

(A) 主要メディア	(B) 社会的な対話インフラ	(C) 使用頻度の高い利用者
(D) 社会的責任	(E) 偽りのニュース	(F) 公益

Learning Important Expressions for Business Case Studies

ビジネスケースの理解に重要な表現に関連する下記の英文を完成させましょう。

1. In Japan, users can tweet a message of ------- 140 characters.

    (A) a lot of   (B) a variety of   (C) a maximum of   (D) a hundred of

2. Twitter users were ------- following famous people's tweets,

    (A) most   (B) mostly   (C) at most   (D) the most

3. The more people use Twitter, the more issues the company seems to -------.

    (A) head   (B) look   (C) hand   (D) face

Listening Booster

企業情報に関する英文を聞いて背景を理解しましょう。

 2-54

A. Listen and choose the best answer to each question.

1. How many people use Twitter in Japan?

    (A) More than 140 an hour

    (B) More than 2,020 a day

    (C) More than 45 million

    (D) More than 321 million

2. Which statement is NOT correct about their conversation?

    (A) The man uses Twitter very often.

    (B) They only talk about the benefits of the social media.

    (C) The man describes the motto of the company.

    (D) Twitter also needs to pay attention to protecting the public interest.

B. Listening Review

Aの音声をもう一度聞き下の英文の（　　　）に適切な表現を書き入れましょう。   2-55

A: It's said that globally, there were more than 321 million [1](　　　　　　) Twitter users in 2020. Do you often use Twitter?

B: Of course. I can't imagine my life without the social media. I love to send short messages within 140 [2](　　　　　).

A: I see. But as the number of Twitter users grows, it has a greater social [3](　　　　　), both positively and negatively.

117

B: I agree, because there are now more than 45 million people using Twitter in Japan. Now, their motto is to "ensure all people can participate in public conversation freely and ⁴(   )."

A: They must keep a balance between enhancing free conversations and protecting the public interest.

B: To achieve such goals, they have set up ⁵(   ) and policies for users and try to judge the relevance of posted information accordingly.

Learning From Authentic Business Examples

Twitter に関するビジネス記事の読んで後の問いに答えましょう。　 2-56～58

Tech World	**Subscribe**

Menu

Under-developing Social Communication Infrastructure

In the beginning, when people first started using Twitter, users were mostly following famous people's tweets, exchanging personal messages with friends, or reporting what they saw nearby. This usage trend changed in 2011 because of the Great East Japan Earthquake. At
5 that time, many types of social infrastructure, including telephone networks, were seriously damaged. Consequently, many people lost the ability to communicate with telephones or computers. However, Twitter and some other social media services were still available. This meant that people could use them to find vital information and
10 communicate with others. This led to Twitter being recognized as an important example of social communication infrastructure.

Moreover, through Twitter, people could learn about transportation service disruptions or accidents quicker than through major media sources, such as TV or radio. People now understand how Twitter gets
15 information to users so quickly. Therefore, many politicians, governments, and public institutions are also using it.

Unfortunately, the more people use Twitter, the more issues the company seems to face. This is because the advantage of being able to tweet anytime and anywhere means that users can post both true and
20 false information that may or may not be checked for authenticity. In

---

fact, the number of false or misleading posts has been increasing recently, and the few editors the company has could not keep up with the demand for reliability checks. As a result, Twitter was unable to discourage dishonest users from posting fake news or content that hurts others.

Notes

· **tweet** Twitter上にメッセージを載せること　 · **authenticity** 信憑性

本文の内容として正しい場合は T を、正しくない場合は F を（ ）に書きましょう。

1. Now, Twitter users tend to follow famous people and entertainers exclusively. (　　)

2. Politicians realize the effectiveness of Twitter for their campaigns. 　　(　　)

3. Audiences have recently been very careful about fake news on social media. 　(　　)

Reading Booster

Twitter のビジネスケースを読んで質問に答えましょう。　　　　CD 2-59～62

Twitter Evolution From Users in Japan

　　　Twitter usage in Japan has been beneficial for the company. This is because the Japanese tend to initiate new Twitter usages that have beneficial purposes. Some of these usages have led to the development of new business opportunities. However, because Japanese Twitter users tend to tweet a lot of information about their daily lives, the company has needed to address problems related to the risks of people becoming 5 too personal and too attached to Twitter.

　　　Mr. Yu Sasamoto became CEO of Twitter Japan in 2014. Prior to this, he had been a leader in the media and IT industries, having worked for companies such as MTV and Microsoft. Under his leadership, Twitter's MAU (Monthly Active Users) reached a high of 45 million in 2017. In fact, Japan has the second highest number of 10 users in the world, while revenue from Japan was more than 14 percent of the total for the company in the third quarter of the 2020 fiscal year. Moreover, Jack Dorsey, the co-founder of Twitter, appreciates the feedback from the Japanese market and the implications this market has for the growth of the company, Accordingly, Sasamoto was promoted to Vice President of Client Solutions for Twitter, Inc in 2016. 15

In 2017, Twitter planned to change their 140-character limit to 280 because many Western customers wanted to make longer posts. However, Sasamoto successfully convinced the headquarters to let Japan keep the limit by providing research data that showed Japanese usage customs and by explaining the cultural context. That is, Japanese
20 users had got used to posting short messages of less than 140 characters. Another uniquely Japanese aspect that Sasamoto highlighted is that the Japanese use Twitter videos very frequently, which accounted for more than half of Twitter Japan's annual revenue in 2020.

Sasamoto also took initiatives to enhance Twitter's social responsibilities based
25 on the company's experiences in Japan. This was because Twitter was occasionally used for bullying or causing suicide attempts. To deal with these problems, Twitter Japan worked with the Japanese government. As a result, Twitter created a service where information popped up when keywords, like suicide were searched for. The information was about how to find help such as suicide prevention lifelines. Additionally, Twitter
30 introduced a feature that allows users to control who can reply to their posts to let them feel safe without worrying about abuse on social media.

Notes

· **MTV** 主に音楽のビデオクリップを放映する放送局
· **MAU (Monthly Active Users)** ソーシャル・メディアなどの使用頻度の基準となる月々の利用者数
· **the third quarter of the 2020 fiscal year** 2020 年度の会計第 3 四半期
· **Vice President of Client Solutions** 顧客問題担当副社長
· **140-character limit to 280** 140 字の制限を 280 字に
· **bullying or causing suicide attempts** いじめや自殺行為を誘発する
· **suicide prevention lifeline** 自殺防止の電話

1. Why has the Japanese market been beneficial for Twitter?

   (A) Because Japanese people find creative ways to use Twitter.

   (B) Because Japanese users avoid sharing personal information.

   (C) Because Japanese people know how to avoid becoming attached to Twitter.

   (D) Because Japanese people are good at avoiding risks.

2. What is NOT one of Mr. Sasamoto's achievements?

   (A) Helping Twitter get a record number of MAU

   (B) Having Twitter keep its character limits

   (C) Getting Twitter to work with MTV

   (D) Explaining the video sharing habits of Japanese users

3. What did Twitter do to improve its social responsibility?

    (A) It stopped suicides.

    (B) It caused bullying to increase.

    (C) It created a safe space for users.

    (D) It provided suicide support information.

> ## Tasks for Business Studies

A Business Focus: ビジネス英語を学ぼう！

> **Social Responsibility as the Significant Communication Platform**
> ユーザー数の増加に伴い、コミュニケーションのプラットフォームとして Twitter の
> 社会への影響力は大きい。発言の自由と公共の利益のバランスを保つためのポリシー
> を明確にし、それを適応する使用ルールを設定している。

B ビジネス英語の理解を深めよう！

Social Networking Service に関する以下の例文を与えられた文字に続くように空所をうめて完成
させましょう。この際、本文を再度確認し、関連する他の事象にも下線を引き **C** のタスクにも活用
できるようにしましょう。

1. There are more than 321 million active Twitter (*u*   ) because it is very
    (*e*   ) to send a short (*m*   ) within 140 characters.

2. People can use the social media to find (*v*   ) information and
    (*c*   ) with others in the social communication (*i*   ).

3. Twitter was unable to (*d*   ) dishonest users from posting (*f*   )
    news or content that (*h*   ) others.

C Business Discussion

B の表現を参考にして、次のテーマについてクラスメートと話し合いましょう。

Social Networking Service (SNS) and its Impact on Society

1. Which social media do you often use and why?

_____

_____

_____

2. What are some benefits to using social media?

_____

_____

_____

3. What are some problems with social media services?

_____

_____

_____

Uniting the World for a Better Tomorrow

Chapter 14

IC Net Limited

IC Net Limited
アイ・シー・ネット株式会社

IC Net is a development consultancy that aims to make the world a better place. It has implemented projects to solve various problems in developing countries and poor regions.

　アイ・シー・ネット社は（株）学研ホールディングスのグループ会社として、世界の開発途上国が直面する様々な課題のコンサルタント業務に取り組んでいる。主に日本の政府開発援助（ODA）を基に、貧困や安全、公衆衛生など開発途上国を良くするための支援者、助言者として活動している。

アイ・シー・ネット社は **ODA** コンサルティング事業を中心に、世界の開発途上国が直面する様々な課題に取り組んできた。中でもバングラディッシュは様々な課題を抱えている。仏教国のミャンマーに住んでいたイスラム教徒のロヒンギャ人は、市民権や選挙権を制限され差別を受けていた。2017 年のミャンマー軍とロヒンギャ武装勢力の紛争により、隣国のバングラディッシュに大量のロヒンギャ難民が押し寄せた。難民を受け入れた村では、元々住んでいた住民の生活が脅かされている。彼らの中でも特に女性が世帯主となっている家庭は貧しい。このような女性が経済的に自立でき、安心して子供たちを育てることができるようにする方法を模索した。

▶ **Warm-up**

写真に関する英文を聞き学習の準備をしましょう。最も適切な選択肢を選びましょう。 🎧 2-63

(A)　　(B)　　(C)　　(D)

▶ **Vocabulary Input**

次の英語に合う日本語を選び記号で答えましょう。 🎧 2-64

1. development consultancy 　　（　　）

2. pasture 　　（　　）

3. refugee 　　（　　）

4. displaced area 　　（　　）

5. many forms of discrimination 　　（　　）

6. become insecure 　　（　　）

7. farmland 　　（　　）

8. livestock 　　（　　）

9. host community 　　（　　）

(A) 避難地域　　(B) 開発コンサルタント　　(C) 家畜　　(D) 治安の悪化する

(E) 難民を受け入れるコミュニティ　　(F) 牧草地　　(G) 様々な差別

(H) 難民　　(I) 農地

ビジネスケースの理解に重要な表現に関連する下記の英文を完成させましょう。

1. They have implemented projects to solve ------- problems in developing countries.

   (A) few   (B) little   (C) much   (D) various

2. These refugees have been ------- to many forms of discrimination.

   (A) subject   (B) subjective   (C) subjecting   (D) subjected

3. The goats can be sold ------- there is a need for cash income.

   (A) however   (B) whoever   (C) whenever   (D) whatever

> ## Listening Booster

企業情報に関する英文を聞いて背景を理解しましょう。　🎧 2-65

A. Listen and choose the best answer to each question.

1. When was IC Net founded?

   (A) In 1920

   (B) In 1970

   (C) In 1993

   (D) In 2017

2. What does the company want to do?

   (A) to develop a consultancy

   (B) to make the world a better place

   (C) to solve all of the problems in developed countries

   (D) to increase overseas offices

B. Listening Review

Aの音声をもう一度聞き下の英文の（　　　）に適切な表現を書き入れましょう。　🎧 2-66

Making a Better Place for Sustainable Development

IC Net Limited is a [1](　　　　　) consultancy that was founded in 1993. IC Net wants to make the world a better place. Accordingly, it has implemented projects to solve various problems in developing countries and poor regions. The projects have been [2](　　　　　) out in more than 120 countries. Additionally, the consultancy's projects have benefitted from much international ³(   ). IC Net was capitalized at 70 million yen and had sales of 2.9 billion yen in 2017. The company employs 162 people and has overseas offices in Thailand, Cambodia, Laos, Bangladesh, Kenya, and the United States. In 2019, it ⁴(   ) the Gakken Holdings Group, Inc., and hopes to continue expanding.

► Learning From Authentic Business Examples ▮▮▮

IC Net に関するビジネス記事の英文を読んで後の問いに答えましょう。　 2-67～69

SDGs Journal

Negative Impact of Rohingya Refugees on the Host Communities in Bangladesh

Because of a clash between the Myanmar army and Rohingya armed groups in 2017, many Rohingya fled to neighboring Bangladesh. Now, Cox's Bazar Province in Bangladesh is home to more than 1 million Rohingya refugees from Myanmar and became one of the most displaced areas in the world in 2020.

5　The Rohingya problem has made problems for others as well. Because the Rohingya live in huge refugee camps, they have negatively affected the lives of the local Bangladeshi. Initially, the locals tried to help the refugees as a host community, but the number of refugees was too large. For example, in one area, about 650,000 Rohingya refugees came to live, which is much more than the 38,000 local

10　residents. As a result, the residents lost their fields, jobs, and the prices of goods increased. In addition, the area has become insecure, and the locals suffer from infectious diseases and poor hygiene problems.

Fortunately for the Bangladeshi, many organizations, including the United Nations, are trying to help. Naoko Inada of IC Net wanted her company to support

15　the Bangladeshi, and they have carefully investigated the current situation and found several serious problems. One of the biggest problems is that much of the land that used to be used for farmland is now being used as a place of residence for the refugees. Thus, farmers cannot grow crops. Moreover, many households keep livestock such as cattle to supplement their livelihoods. However, the

20　establishment of refugee camps resulted in a significant loss of pasture.

· **Rohingya** ミャンマーに居住していたムスリム教徒の一種族
· **Cox's Bazar Province** バングラデシュのミャンマー国境にあるコックスバザール県
· **infectious diseases and poor hygiene problems** 伝染病と衛生問題

本文の内容として正しい場合は T を、正しくない場合は F を（　）に書きましょう。

1. People in Cox's Bazar Province asked for help from the World Health Organization to
receive more refugees.　　　　　　　　　　　　　　　　　　　　（　　）

2. Rohingya started living in a place where they have Bangladeshi relatives.　（　　）

3. Refugee camps decreased the number of visiting people.　　　　　（　　）

Reading Booster

IC Net のビジネスケースを読んで質問に答えましょう。　　　　　CD 2-70〜74

Improvement of Livelihood in the Host Communities Through Goat Bank

　　　The refugees who worked for lower wages caused Bangladeshi residents in the
host community to lose work and income. Among them, female-headed households
(FHH) were greatly impacted. Inada realized the need for such women to be financially
independent and able to raise their children.

　　　IC Net thought of using goats to enhance the life of the host community. This　5
is because female goats usually give birth every six months to one year, and the goats
can be sold whenever there is a need for cash income. Therefore, IC Net decided to use
the Goat Bank mutual aid system.

　　　First, IC Net chose a local women's group, including FHH, and lets them help
each other. They consist of 100 members, and IC Net offers 50 female and several male　10
goats to the group.　Then, IC Net offers careful instruction on how to raise the goats.
The group decides the order in which the female goats will be given out. A member who

receives a female goat is obliged to give one of the offspring to the next member who has never received one. By doing this, the women in the host communities can support each
15 other and their families. This means that support from organizations can be reduced.

IC Net needed to raise the funds to start the program. To do this, Inada used a web-based crowdfunding platform to raise the initial project money. She presented an attractive plan to enable Bangladesh women to become independent through the Goat Bank. The project successfully collected more than 2.23 million yen from 131 supporters.
20 IC Net used the fund to start the program and hold workshops to organize the bank and raise goats. Little by little, the Goat Bank succeeded, and the Bangladeshi women were able to improve their families' lives. Finally, the Livelihood Improvement for Enhancing Resilience in Host-communities project in Cox's Bazar was officially accepted as a JICA Partnership Program in 2018. IC Net has been at the head of this
25 official project since May 2019 and supports 640 households in the host community.

Notes
· **female-headed households (FHH)** 女性を世帯主とする世帯　· **financially independent** 経済的自立
· **crowdfunding** インターネット上で出資者を募り活動資金を募る
· **JICA Partnership Program** JICA の支援する協力事業

1. What caused the Bangladeshi residents in the host community to lose work and income?
   (A) a lack of government donations
   (B) not enough banks
   (C) refugees who will work for less money
   (D) having too many children

2. Why are goats a good way to help the host community?
   (A) because they produce a lot of babies
   (B) because they drink a lot of milk
   (C) because local women's groups know a lot about goats
   (D) because goats are very expensive

3. What must a person do with the offspring of a goat?
   (A) eat the goat
   (B) play with the goat
   (C) help refugees
   (D) donate the goat to another member

A Business Focus: ビジネス英語を学ぼう！

ODA and JICA

JICA は日本の政府開発援助（ODA: Office Development Assistance）を具体的に実施する機関の窓口のとなり、様々な支援事業を行っている。これらの支援事業の実施は多くの場合、経験豊富な IC Net などの開発コンサルタント企業が受託する。

Goat Bank

ヤギは育てやすく、必要時には容易に現金化できる。地元で協力しあうコミュニティを形成してもらい、ヤギをもらった家に最初のメスが生まれたら、それを順番に与える。このようにヤギを飼育することで生活の安定を目指す。

B ビジネス英語の理解を深めよう！

Host communityに関する以下の例文を与えられた文字に続くように空所をうめて完成させましょう。この際、本文を再度確認し、関連する他の事象にも下線を引き **C** のタスクにも活用できるようにしましょう。

1. The number of refugees was too (l), so the residents in the host community lost their (f) and jobs, and the prices of goods (i).

2. It is necessary for female-headed (h) in the community to be financially (i) and able to raise their (c).

3. IC Net decided to use the (G) Bank mutual aid system so that the (w) in the host communities can (s) each other and their families.

C Business Discussion

Bの表現を参考にして、次のテーマについてクラスメートと話し合いましょう。

1. What are the problems faced by the host community in Cox's Bazar Province?

_____

_____

_____

2. What did Inada realize about the host community?

_____

_____

_____

3. What kind of solutions were used to improve the situation of the host community?

_____

_____

_____

Developing a Mobile Platform

Mongolia introduced a multi-party system in 1990 and abandoned socialism. The average GDP (Gross Domestic Product) was around 140th in the world in 1995.

　住友商事（株）は日本の4大総合商社の1つで世界65の国と地域でビジネスを行っている。950のグループ会社を持ち、従業員は7万2千人以上である。新興国モンゴルは人口が少なく、国民総生産も低く、市場としては小さい。だが住友商事は、携帯電話がまだ普及していなかったモンゴルで事業を開始することにした。住友商事の2020年度の売上高は13,820億円で、営業利益は1,756億円を記録している。

Business Issue 新興国モンゴルでコミュニケーションネットワークを構築

　モンゴルは日本の約4倍の国土の広さに、日本の約40分の1の329万人ほどしか住んでいない。このため外国企業が参入するには市場が小さく、日本企業にとっても進出する国として優先順位は低い。外交的に重要な位置にあるモンゴルの経済発展のためにも、携帯電話の普及を日本企業が促進することは意義があった。しかし、全く基盤のない規模の小さな市場でどうやって事業を軌道に乗せればよいのか、住友商事の藤原は戦略を練っていた。

Warm-up

写真に関する英文を聞き学習の準備をしましょう。最も適切な選択肢を選びましょう。　2-75

(A)　　(B)　　(C)　　(D)

Vocabulary Input

次の英語に合う日本語を選び記号で答えましょう。　2-76

1. general trading company　（　　　）
2. phone subscribers　（　　　）
3. solicit　（　　　）
4. multi-party system　（　　　）
5. economic diplomacy　（　　　）
6. stable supply　（　　　）
7. GDP　（　　　）
8. higher-ups　（　　　）

(A) 経済外交	(B) 安定供給	(C) 国内総生産	(D) 勧誘する
(E) 会社の上層部	(F) 複数政党制	(G) 電話加入者	(H) 総合商社

ビジネスケースの理解に重要な表現に関連する下記の英文を完成させましょう。

1. Major companies attempted to ------- to Mongolia's economic development.

   (A) contribute   (B) combine   (C) constitute   (D) compromise

2. This old equipment became ------- date as soon as modern IT technologies advanced.

   (A) up to   (B) leave off   (C) out of   (D) as to

3. The service was launched in the capital city, ------- many people live.

   (A) there   (B) how   (C) which   (D) where

Listening Booster

ビジネスケースに関する英文を聞いて背景を理解しましょう。 2-77

A. Listen and choose the best answer to each question.

1. Who is the guest speaker?

   (A) A student

   (B) Professor Davis

   (C) Mr. Fujiwara

   (D) Ms. Huston

2. According to the speaker, what is the role of general trading companies?

   (A) working on economic diplomacy

   (B) securing a stable supply of resources

   (C) supporting the overseas expansion of Japanese companies

   (D) expanding global business networks

B. Listening Review

Ａの音声をもう一度聞き下の英文の（　　　）に適切な表現を書き入れましょう。 2-78

Welcome to this lecture series of business case studies. My name is Professor Jack Davis of the Economics Department. Before introducing our guest speaker, Mr. Hiroto Fujiwara of Sumitomo Corporation, let me explain the role of major ¹(　　　　　) companies in Japan. Ms. Lucy Huston will give you the pamphlet of the companies afterward. First of all, in order to achieve strong ²(　　　　　) for the Japanese economy, the Japanese government works on economic diplomacy, such as supporting the overseas expansion of Japanese companies and securing a stable supply of ³(　　　　　). To enhance such strategies, general trading companies have played a significant role in expanding global business ⁴(　　　　　).

> ### Learning From Authentic Business Examples ▮▮▮

住友商事のビジネスケースに関する次の雑誌記事を読んで後の問いに答えましょう。 2-79,80

Business Perspectives

Toward Building a Strategic Partnership with Mongolia

In 1995, the Mongolian government solicited foreign companies to help develop their telecommunications industry and provide support for future infrastructure needs. However, because of the small market size and country risks, few major players from the telecommunications industry were eager to join the
5 project. Nevertheless, the Telecommunication Department of Sumitomo Corporation attempted to enter this business. This is because it wanted to develop a new business model. Previously, Sumitomo had been exporting large and expensive telecommunication equipment overseas. Unfortunately, this equipment became out of date as soon as modern mobile phone technologies advanced.
10 Due to the small size of the Mongolian market, it might have seemed difficult to convince the higher-ups at Sumitomo Corporation to agree to the project. The Mongolian population was about 2.3 million, and the GDP per capita was $695 US dollars in 1994. Moreover, mobile devices cost about US $300, which was too

expensive for ordinary Mongolians. On the other hand, as this was a national project, the Mongolian government promised favorable conditions to Sumitomo, such as granting it exclusivity for the first five years. Also, for the first five years there would be no corporate tax, and for the following five years, the tax would be half the normal amount. As a result of these incentives, Sumitomo's project team made a business plan to increase the number of mobile phone subscribers to 5,000 in three years and turn a profit.

15

20

Notes

· **telecommunication department** 通信事業部 · **GDP per capita** 一人当たり国民総生産
· **favorable conditions** 優遇措置 · **exclusivity** ビジネスの独占 · **incentives** インセンティブ
· **turn a profit** 黒字化

本文の内容として正しい場合は T を、正しくない場合は F を（　）に書きましょう。

1. Few major players from the telecommunications industry were eager to join the project because of the small market size and country risks. 　　　　　　（　　）

2. Sumitomo had been exporting modern mobile phone technologies overseas. （　　）

3. The Mongolian government promised to increase the number of mobile phone subscribers to 5,000 in three years. 　　　　　　（　　）

Reading Booster

住友商事のビジネスケースを読んで質問に答えましょう。　　　　　　CD 2-81〜84

Expanding Communication Infrastructure Under Unpredictable Conditions

In 1995, Sumitomo Corporation's joint proposal was selected for the first mobile phone business project in Mongolia through a process of joint bidding. To promote this business, MobiCom Corporation, with capital of US $9 million, was set up in 1995. Sumitomo Corporation invested US $4 million, and KDD also invested. A local company, NewCom, was supposed to invest US $1 million, but it did not have enough financial resources for the investment. Therefore, Sumitomo loaned the company the funds. NewCom was expected to help them successfully negotiate with the government, local suppliers, and residents.

In 1996, the service was launched in Ulaanbaatar, the capital city, where about half of the population lives. Despite the high price of mobile phones for local people,

5

10

the demand was unexpectedly high, and the business went well. Initially, they expected to acquire 5,000 users in three years to become profitable. However, they exceeded the target and became profitable from the first year.

15   Mr. Hiroto Fujiwara took over the business in 1997, and the company launched regional cellular communications. The contract with the Mongolian government was supposed to have zero corporate income tax for five years. However, because of MobiCom's unexpected success, the tax office suddenly decided to charge corporate taxes from year two. Fujiwara faced difficulties in his negotiations to carry out the tax-free conditions. Surprisingly, on the day just before an official visit to Japan by Mongolian
20 President Bagabandi in 1998, the tax office informed Fujiwara of the cancellation of the country's tax claim from year two.

     The business venture seemed like it would go well because the contract promised that Mongolia would not allow any new competitors to enter this market for the first five years. However, in 1999, the Korean company Skytel got a license to launch its
25 mobile business there. Against all these difficulties, Mobicom expanded its business and made Mongolia's Top 100 Companies list in 2019, and in 2020, Mobicom had more than one million users, which is a 40 percent share of the market.

Notes

· **joint bidding** 共同入札   · **capital** 資本金   · **KDD** 国際電信電話株式会社（現在の KDDI 前身会社の一つ）
· **loan the funds** 資金を貸与する   · **regional cellular communication** 地方の携帯通話
· **tax-free conditions** 無税の条件   · **official visit** 公式訪問

1. How much money did Sumitomo Corporation use to set up operations in Mongolia?

   (A) US $9 million   (B) US $4 million

   (C) US $5 million   (D) US $1 million

2. What happened during Sumitomo Corporation's first year of business?

   (A) They acquired more than 5,000 users.

   (B) They sold mobile phones to half of the population.

   (C) They did not make any profit.

   (D) They could not attract enough users.

3. Why did the Mongolian government want to charge Sumitomo Corporation income tax from 1997?

   (A) Because the President of Mongolia was going to visit Japan.

   (B) Because Sumitomo was so successful at business in 1996.

   (C) Because MobiCom was having financial trouble.

   (D) Because Skytel was coming to Mongolia.

Tasks for Business Studies

A Business Focus: ビジネス英語を学ぼう！

Economic and Technical Assistance for the Development of Emerging Countries

総合商社は日本の経済外交政策において、国際貿易の促進や企業の海外進出、市場開拓の重要な役割を担ってきた。

Taking Various Risks in Emerging Countries

新興国のビジネスは政情不安や政治家の権限乱用で様々なリスクを抱えることもある。

B ビジネス英語の理解を深めよう！

モンゴルのビジネスに関する以下の例文を与えられた文字に続くように空所をうめて完成させましょう。この際、本文を再度確認し、関連する他の事象にも下線を引き C のタスクにも活用できるようにしましょう。

1. It wanted to (*d*   ) a new business (*m*   ) because its main (*e*   ) became out of date.

2. The Mongolian (*g*   ) decided to change the (*c*   ) for zero corporate (*i*   ) tax for five years.

3. The (*K*   ) company Skytel got a (*l*   ) to launch its (*m*   ) business.

C Business Discussion

Bの表現を参考にして、次のテーマについてクラスメートと話し合いましょう。

1. Why did Sumitomo Corporation decided to launch a telecommunication business in Mongolia?

   _____

   _____

   _____

   _____

2. What kind of problems has Sumitomo Corporation faced?

   _____

   _____

   _____

   _____

Review Unit 4

1 最も適切な応答の選択肢を選びましょう。 2-85～88

Listen to the question or statement and three responses. Then choose the best answer.

1. (A) (B) (C)

2. (A) (B) (C)

3. (A) (B) (C)

4. (A) (B) (C)

2 ビジネスケースを復習しよう！

E-mail

To: Paul Davis
From: Jenny Hopkins
Subject: Water business
Date: December 23

Dear Paul

I wish you the best for the Christmas holidays and hope my report on Yamaha Motor unique business finds you well.

As I mentioned above, Yamaha Motor has created an interesting water business in developing countries, and as I remember, you are always looking for creative water business models, so I thought I should report on what I learned.
Originally, Yamaha Motor developed a home-use water ------- system for
1
Japanese families who were sent to Indonesia. The system called OH 300 was able to improve poor drinking water for the Japanese or the rich in developing countries.

However, half of the local ------- who worked for Yamaha Motor in developing
2

countries often live in villages, which have no public water services. They live in ------- conditions and only have access to river water. Unfortunately, OH
3
300,worked well for tap water, but not dirty river water. Finally, in 2000s, Yamaha Motor developed Yamaha Clean Water Supply System. ------- In
4
2020, 41 YCWSs were successfully operating to improve peoples' lives with clean water in 14 different countries in Asia and Africa. I hope you are interested in this report. Please feel free to ask me any questions about their business model.

Best regards,
Jenny

1. (A) sustainable
   (B) purification
   (C) generating
   (D) mixing

2. (A) farmers
   (B) suppliers
   (C) agents
   (D) employees

3. (A) healthy
   (B) pessimistic
   (C) unsanitary
   (D) tolerable

4. (A) JETRO helped the company to develop the technology.
   (B) People can have enough hot water to survive in villages.
   (C) Japanese families helped the local people who have water problems.
   (D) The system can clean the surface water from rivers and lakes.

3 3つの文章を読み最も適切な選択肢を選びましょう。

Proposal for JICA : Improvement of Livelihood Through Goat Bank

Overview of the Project

- **Major support and activities : Goat raising and vegetable production**

- **Budget : Approx. 80,000USD through ODA**

- **Project period : September 2021– January 2022**

Slide No. 4

E-mail

To: Sakurako Urashima
From: Jack Dorset
Subject: Inquiry about your presentation slide
Date: July 4

Dear Ms. Urashima.

Thank you for sending me your slides for the proposal. They seem fine in general.

However, I have some questions about Slide No. 4. Could you answer the following questions?

1. How will the Goat Bank be organized?
2. What are ODA and JICA?

I think it is better to make this clear for your audience.

Best regards,
Jack Dorset

```
                              E-mail
        To:  Sakurako Urashima
      From:  Jack Dorset
   Subject:  Re: Inquiry about your presentation slide
      Date:  July 5
```

Dear Mr. Dorset,

Thank you for checking my English and inquiring about my slides.

Here is my reply to your questions.

1. The local women's groups can play a central role in managing the goat bank. For example, they manage the number of goats received, record the births of offspring, goat returns, etc.

2. ODA is the government funding agency that provides financial assistance to developing countries to promote socioeconomic development. Aspects of the funding that are controlled by JICA are Technical Cooperation, Japanese ODA Loans, and Grant Aid.

I hope these answers make sense to you.

Best regards,
Sakurako Urashima

---

1. In which month will the project end?

(A) July (B) September (C) December (D) January

2. What is the purpose of the first e-mail?

(A) correcting Ms. Urashima's English

(B) making facts about the audience clear

(C) asking some questions

(D) confirming the purpose of the presentation

3. What is NOT a role of local women's groups?

(A) managing the number of goats received

(B) recording the births of goats

(C) managing the goat bank

(D) receiving financial assistance

TEXT PRODUCTION STAFF

edited by	編集
Eiichi Tamura	田村 栄一

cover design by	表紙デザイン
Nobuyoshi Fujino	藤野 伸芳

text design by	本文デザイン
Hiroyuki Kinouchi(ALIUS)	木野内 宏行 (アリウス)

CD PRODUCTION STAFF

narrated by	吹き込み者
Howard Colefield (AmerE)	ハワード・コルフィールド (アメリカ英語)
Karen Haedrich (AmerE)	カレン・ヘドリック (アメリカ英語)

Global Business Case Studies
グローバルリーダーに学ぶビジネス戦略

2023年1月20日　初版発行
2024年2月15日　第3刷発行

著　　者　中谷 安男
　　　　　Ryan Smithers

発 行 者　佐野 英一郎

発 行 所　株式会社 成 美 堂
　　　　　〒101-0052　東京都千代田区神田小川町3-22
　　　　　TEL 03-3291-2261　FAX 03-3293-5490
　　　　　https://www.seibido.co.jp

印 刷・製 本　萩原印刷株式会社

ISBN 978-4-7919-7266-1　　　　　　　　　　　Printed in Japan